The Palgrave Kets de Vries Library

Manfred F. R. Kets de Vries, Distinguished Professor of Leadership and Development and Organizational Change at INSEAD, is one of the world's leading thinkers on leadership, coaching, and the application of clinical psychology to individual and organizational change.

Palgrave's professional business list operates at the interface between academic rigor and real-world implementation. Professor Kets de Vries's work exemplifies that perfect combination of intellectual depth and practical application and Palgrave is proud to bring almost a decade's worth of work together in the Palgrave Kets de Vries Library.

More information about this series at
http://www.palgrave.com/gp/series/16661

Manfred F. R. Kets de Vries

Quo Vadis?

The Existential Challenges of Leaders

Manfred F. R. Kets de Vries
Europe Campus
INSEAD
FONTAINEBLEAU, France

ISSN 2730-7581 ISSN 2730-759X (electronic)
The Palgrave Kets de Vries Library
ISBN 978-3-030-66701-6 ISBN 978-3-030-66699-6 (eBook)
https://doi.org/10.1007/978-3-030-66699-6

This Palgrave Macmillan imprint is published by the registered company Springer Nature Switzerland AG.
The registered company address is: Gewerbestrasse 11, 6330 Cham, Switzerland

Preface

Life and death have been lacking in my life.

—*Jorge Luis Borges*

Sleep is lovely, death is better still, not to have been born is of course the miracle.

—*Heinrich Heine*

I recently had lunch with a very old friend. It was a special occasion as we hadn't seen each other for a long time. We talked about our children. We talked about our work. We talked about our wellbeing. My friend told me that he recently had to deal with a number of health issues. He sighed, "Aging is difficult." In response, I couldn't help quoting Bette Davis' famous statement that "Getting old is not for sissies." I went on, "Someone once told me that if you feel pain when you wake up in the morning, it's a good sign. It means you're still alive." Taking a cue from my comments, my friend said that he had been to five funerals this year, and that one of his old work colleagues was now suffering from dementia. That led to my telling him that during the past year, I had also lost two people close to me.

As the waiter refilled our glasses, I thought about those two funerals. I would never be able to reminiscence with those friends in the way I was doing with my friend that day. I was reminded of the words of Gustave Flaubert, "A friend who dies, it's something of you who dies." I was suddenly filled with sadness at the thought of the tragic transience of things. Every week, in the newspapers or on the news, the obituaries of people who had been part of my cultural and socio-economic landscape stared me in the face.

I looked out of the window of the restaurant. The leaves were dropping from the trees. Dandelion seeds were blowing in the wind. A flock of geese flew overhead. The fall was making its entry, the birds were going south, and another year had gone by. It was a further reminder of life's temporariness. As I got older, time was passing more and more quickly. I was miserably aware of the dark cloud of death hanging over me.

The mood at our lunch table had suddenly changed.

Every year, I run a seminar for C-suite executives. The objective is to help them to become more effective and reflective leaders, and the usual topics focus on leadership and career issues. In reality, however, the seminar casts a much broader net than this. For most participants, the seminar is a starting point for a journey into the self, unearthing layers and layers of memories that have lain hidden for a very long time.

I liken this process to peeling an onion: one layer at the time. As they embark on this journey of introspection, the participants obtain greater insights into what they're all about, why they do what they do, and what makes them the people they are. My hope is that they will gain a better understanding of how the ghosts of their past influence their present, and can have an impact on their future. Step by step, over the course of the workshop, leadership and career issues give way to less obvious themes, such as their character, their mental health, the quality of their interpersonal relationships, and future challenges. These reflections become the starting point to make them think about the choices they have made in their lives, the kind of work they do, their interpersonal relationships, their search for meaning in their activities, and the meaning of death. Encouraged by what's happening during the workshop, many of them are now ready to ask themselves questions like: Could I have lived a very different life? And if so, what would such a life have looked like? What are my options for the future? And what am I going to do with the time that's left?

In a very real way, the aim of this seminar is to get the participants to address the age-old question, "Quo vadis?"—"Where are you going?" The expression refers to a story about Saint Peter, one of the twelve Apostles of Christ and the first leader of the early Catholic Church. As Peter is fleeing Rome to avoid crucifixion by the emperor Nero, he encounters the risen Christ on the Appian Way. Peter asks Jesus, "Quo vadis?" Jesus replies, "I am going to Rome to be crucified again." The answer gives Peter the courage to return to Rome and continue his ministry.

In his search for meaning, Peter was willing to sacrifice everything for what he believed in. He was trying to deal with the major existential questions that have troubled humankind from the beginning of time: Who am I? What's the meaning of my life? Where are we going? In my work with students, patients, and clients, this always becomes the overriding theme. Strange as it may sound, this search for meaning is intricately connected to the concern about aging and our inevitable death. Most of us, to take a well-used expression, want to die young as late as possible. Death is our constant companion but at the same time—perhaps paradoxically—the certainty of death encourages us to search for meaning in life. Given the ubiquity of these concerns in every area of my professional life, I decided to write directly about them. I hope this book will give the readers some food for thought and help them cope with the knowledge that everything in our existence is temporary. All of us have to accept that it is our mortality and transience that make our lives such a bitter-sweet experience. And with the present pandemic plaguing the world, these reflections have become even more salient. With so many people dying, death has become an even closer reality.

Paris, France
March 1, 2021

Manfred F. R. Kets de Vries

Praise for *Quo Vadis?*

"*Quo Vadis?* is not just a book about leadership, it reaches far beyond. The book is relevant for anyone who thinks about life and that there will be an end. Manfred Kets de Vries gives context and explains the key role of meaning in encountering death anxiety by linking it to happiness, purpose, motivation, health (and free will). He reminds us that no demagogue or religious leader can simply give us meaning. In the end, we have to create meaning for ourselves."

—Christoph Loch, *Professor of Operations and Technology Management, Dean at Cambridge Judge Business School, University of Cambridge*

"The purpose of most management literature is to make you feel smart and confident by confirming and articulating thoughts you already have had. This book is very different. Manfred Kets de Vries is a brave person and writer. Reading *Quo Vadis?*, perhaps the most poignant of all his books, is taking a risk. The risk of being challenged and changed as a leader, manager, and human being, in a way you have not been prepared for."

—Ulf Lockowandt, MD, PhD, *Associate Professor of Surgery, Karolinska Institute, Consultant Cardiothoracic Surgeon, EMBA Stockholm School of Economics, Head of Division for Special Operations Stockholm Health Care Services*

"*Quo Vadis?* is Manfred Kets de Vries' most profound book yet, challenging not just leaders but every one of us to find our own sweet spot combination of happiness and meaning in life. Every page confronts the reader with past and present choices and what he or she may be running away from. It also provides a guide to finding one's personal goals, stop wasting time on things that don't have meaning, and making the changes which may lead to "a life well lived.""

—Philippe Haspeslagh, *Honorary Dean and Partner Vlerick Business School, President of the Family Business Network Belgium, Chairman of Ardo*

"A fascinating journey of coming to terms with life's final destination. A tour de force from Professor Manfred Kets de Vries, the master of the psychodynamic orientation to management. Drawing on impressive philosophical, literary and scholarly sources, the author offers a unique perspective on handling the inevitability of death with humor, lightness and style. A must read for those considering themselves reflective leaders."

—Stanislav Shekshnia, *Senior Affiliate Professor, INSEAD, France/ Singapore, Senior Partner, Ward Howell International*

“These wide-ranging reflections are extraordinary engaging and erudite. In a captivating tour de force Manfred Kets de Vries revisits life and death, the two things that bind us all. I have not come across a more convincing, irresistibly worded overview of what—on balance—makes the goal of immorbidity worth the efforts. A must-read.”

—Victor Halberstadt, *Professor of Economics, Leiden University*

Contents

About the Author

Manfred F. R. Kets de Vries brings a different view to the much-studied subjects of leadership and the psychological dimensions of individual and organizational change. Bringing to bear his knowledge and experience of economics (Econ. Drs., University of Amsterdam), management (ITP, MBA, and DBA, Harvard Business School), and psychoanalysis (Membership Canadian Psychoanalytic Society, Paris Psychoanalytic Society, and the International Psychoanalytic Association), he explores the interface between management science, psychoanalysis, developmental psychology, evolutionary psychology, neuroscience, psychotherapy, executive coaching, and consulting. His specific areas of interest are leadership (the "bright" and "dark" side), entrepreneurship, career dynamics, talent management, family business, cross-cultural management, succession planning, organizational and individual stress, C-suite team building, executive coaching, organizational development, transformation management, and management consulting.

The Distinguished Clinical Professor of Leadership Development and Organizational Change at INSEAD, he is Program Director of INSEAD's top management program, "The Challenge of Leadership: Creating Reflective Leaders," and the Founder of INSEAD's Executive Master Program in Change Management. As an educator, he has received INSEAD's distinguished teacher award six times. He has held professorships at McGill University, the École des Hautes Études Commerciales, Montreal, the European School for Management and Technology (ESMT), Berlin, and the Harvard Business School. He has lectured at management institutions around the world. *The Financial Times*, *Le Capital*, *Wirtschaftswoche*, and *The Economist* have rated Manfred Kets de Vries among the world's leading management thinkers and among the most influential contributors to human resource management.

Kets de Vries is the author, co-author, or editor of more than 50 books, including *The Neurotic Organization, Leaders, Fools and Impostors, Life and Death in the Executive Fast Lane, The Leadership Mystique, The Happiness Equation, Are Leaders Made or Are They Born? The Case of Alexander the Great, The New Russian Business Elite, Leadership by Terror, The Global Executive Leadership Inventory, The Leader on the Couch, Coach and Couch, The Family Business on the Couch, Sex, Money, Happiness, and Death: The Quest for Authenticity, Reflections on Leadership and Character, Reflections on Leadership and Career, Reflections on Organizations, The Coaching Kaleidoscope, The Hedgehog Effect: The Secrets of High Performance Teams, Mindful Leadership Coaching: Journeys into the Interior, You Will Meet a Tall Dark Stranger: Executive Coaching Challenges* and *Telling Fairy Tales in the Boardroom: How to Make Sure Your Organization Lives Happily Ever After, Riding the Leadership Roller Coaster: A Psychological Observer's Guide, Down the Rabbit Hole of Leadership: Leadership Pathology of Everyday Life, Journeys into Coronavirus Land: Lessons from an Pandemic* and *The CEO Whisperer: Meditations on Leaders, Life and Change.*

In addition, Kets de Vries has published more than four hundred academic papers as chapters in books and as articles (including digital). He has also written more than hundred case studies, including seven that received the Best Case of the Year award. He is a regular writer for various magazines. Furthermore, his work has been featured in such publications as *The New York Times, The Wall Street Journal, The Los Angeles Times, Fortune, Business Week, The Economist, The Financial Times* and *The Harvard Business Review.* His books and articles have been translated into more than thirty languages. He writes regular blogs for the *Harvard Business Review* and *INSEAD Knowledge.* He is a member of seventeen editorial boards and is a Fellow of the Academy of Management. He is also a founding member of the International Society for the Psychoanalytic Study of Organizations (ISPSO), which has honored him as a lifetime member. Kets de Vries is also the first non-US recipient of International Leadership Association Lifetime Achievement Award for his contributions to leadership research and development (being considered one of the world's founding professionals in the development of leadership as a field and discipline). In addition, he received a Lifetime Achievement Award from Germany for his advancement of executive education. The American Psychological Association has honored him with the "Harry and Miriam Levinson Award" for his contributions to Organizational Consultation. Furthermore, he is the recipient of the "Freud Memorial Award" for his work to further the interface between management and psychoanalysis. In addition, he has also received the "Vision of Excellence Award" from the Harvard

Institute of Coaching. Kets de Vries is the first beneficiary of INSEAD's Dominique Héau Award for "Inspiring Educational Excellence." He is also the recipient of two honorary doctorates. The Dutch government has made him an Officer in the Order of Oranje Nassau.

Kets de Vries works as a consultant on organizational design/transformation and strategic human resource management for companies worldwide. As an educator and consultant, he has worked in more than forty countries. In his role as a consultant, he is also the founder-chairman of the Kets de Vries Institute (KDVI), a boutique strategic leadership development consulting firm.

Kets de Vries was the first fly fisherman in Outer Mongolia (at the time, becoming the world record holder of the Siberian hucho taimen). He is a member of New York's Explorers Club. In his spare time, he can be found in the rainforests or savannas of Central and Southern Africa, the Siberian taiga, the Ussuri Krai, Kamchatka, the Pamir and Altai Mountains, Arnhemland, or within the Arctic Circle.

List of Figures

1

The Oldest Question

If we possess a why of life we can put up with almost any how.
—Friedrich Nietzsche
The meaning of life is that it ends.
—Franz Kafka

Working longer and longer hours trying to get his latest start-up up and running, Ted was at rock bottom, questioning the fundamentals of his existence, something to which he had never given much thought. What am I doing with my life? Does it have any purpose? Is there anything I can look forward to? These questions were brought on by his feeling of increasing isolation. Although the company he was leading was growing rapidly, he hadn't felt connected to his co-founders and co-workers for quite some time. His involvement in yet another start-up was bringing him very little satisfaction. Until now he had been too busy with his work and related activities to wonder about the meaning of life. But now he felt lost. The time for reflection due to the pandemic had been a catalyst. Presently, since his children had left home, the hustle and bustle seemed pointless. For some time now, he had been feeling aimless, wondering what he was doing with his life. Somehow, life made less and less sense to him; it even seemed tedious. It had been a long time since he had felt happy. It didn't help that his relationship with his wife was not good. Their marriage had become superficial and lifeless. For too many years, they had both been busy scheduling what needed to be done to make the household work, taking the children to school or to sports events, shopping for household necessities, planning the occasional dinner party. Was that what

M. F. R. Kets de Vries, *Quo Vadis?*, The Palgrave Kets de Vries Library,
https://doi.org/10.1007/978-3-030-66699-6_1

marriage was all about? Shouldn't it be much more? He and his wife now behaved like two old acquaintances who were boarding together. They had very little in common. And sex had been non-existent for a very long time. Ted was in bad physical shape as well, having piled on weight over the past 12 months.

As Ted took stock of his life, he realized that the very foundations of his existence were being shaken. He had been depressed before, but the way he felt now was way beyond what he had experienced on other occasions. It felt like his life had been turned upside down and lost its center. His sense of being isolated in the world had become all-encompassing. He wondered whether he was in the middle of some kind of existential crisis—whatever that meant.

What was happening to him? Should he stop doing what he was doing? But if he lost the defining structure of work, wouldn't he get even more depressed? Ted had lost sight of what he was living for. He found himself thinking more and more about death, with the increasing realization that he wasn't able to face his own mortality.

In the past, the repression of uncomfortable thoughts had always been one of Ted's strengths but now he couldn't push these negative thoughts out of his mind. Obviously, his defenses were no longer working—the nightmares and panic attacks he had begun to have were clear warning signs. But however hard he tried to push these dark thoughts away, the attacks kept returning. The last one had been particularly scary—he could hear his heart pounding, his chest hurt, and he had difficulty breathing.

Ironically enough, never having been religious, Ted had started to envy religious people. At least their faith—their belief that there was a God who looked after them—brought them some comfort. He felt he had nothing to help him with his despair. Everything had seemed so much simpler in the past. Now it seemed as if there was "Record" might be a more illustrative term running through his head, constantly repeating questions: Why am I doing what I'm doing? Is it all work until I drop dead? If I die right now, what difference have I made to the world? Has my time on Earth really been worthwhile? Have I been chasing the wrong things all my life?

Ted felt that he had nobody to turn to, nobody to whom he could talk about his present angst. He was increasingly estranged from his wife, who was far too busy with her own career. So were his children. He had no other family. He was an only child, his parents had died when he was in his early twenties, and he had very few friends. Obsessed with his work, he had done very little to maintain these relationships.

Ted felt his life was no longer his own but was being controlled by external forces. Sometimes, it felt as though things were being done to him. Work had turned into a boring and joyless routine. Getting out of bed in the morning seemed pointless. Every day seemed very much like any other. He was just going through the motions. He thought increasingly about suicide.

What was happening to Ted? Why was such an energetic and driven man feeling so exhausted and purposeless? His dissatisfaction with his work and his failing marriage no doubt contributed to some extent to his unhappiness. Two of the major pillars of human life—love and work—had begun to crumble. His habitual set of defenses against intrusive thoughts about life and death had become ineffective. But more profoundly, Ted was suffering from existential malaise—a fundamental rupture of all his assumptions and actions that made him wonder whether his life had any real meaning, purpose, or value. Generally speaking, this tragic view of life emerges when we have difficulty accepting the finiteness of our existence, the inescapable fact of our death. We'll meet Ted again in Chap. 4.

The Meaning of Life

What is the meaning of life? This question is as old as the span of time Homo sapiens has been on Earth. The search for life's meaning is the uniting characteristic of our species and is perhaps the most important part of being human. Ours is the only species to question whether our life, and anything we do with our life, matters, or has any sort of importance. It might be better to ask, what meaning do we give to our life? Whatever our perspective, dealing with this question is essential to be able to function effectively as a human being.

When I meet people who tell me they live a life that has no or very little meaning, I have noticed that—apart from being confused—they are also generally troubled by various psychological symptoms. Some people may even be suicidal. Given the seriousness of this mental condition, it is unsurprising that throughout the history of humankind, the question of the meaning of life has attracted theologians, philosophers, psychologists, evolutionists, and cosmologists. Homo sapiens, consciously or unconsciously, has always been on a quest for an answer to this question, an attempt to understand the lessons life tries to teach during our temporary existence on Earth.

Of course, Ted is far from being alone with his existential angst. The tragedy of the human condition is a story of how to deal with the terror of death—what kinds of conscious and unconscious defense mechanisms we use to cope with what we know is coming, given that death will always remain a mystery to us. And it is this mystery that creates death anxiety and makes us question life's purpose.

Many of us are quite successful in pushing our feelings of unease into the background. We are experts at using our defenses. Whenever possible, we prefer not to think of death, or at least to pay little conscious attention to its inevitable reality. Perhaps that's the way we are programmed, from an evolutionary perspective. Just as children are frightened of the dark, we fear the prospect of death. We prefer not to think about it. But despite our heroic efforts not to see what we don't want to see, many people experience a generalized feeling of insignificance in the greater scheme of things on a daily basis. It is this recognition of the human condition that makes for the tragic quality of our lives, because ours is also the only species that has to live with the understanding and consciousness of our death.

Due the development of the frontal lobes of our brain—a critical moment in the evolutionary development of our species—we have always been curious about why things are the way they are. This knowledge of the fact of death motivates us to ask the big questions: Why are we here? Why does life end? And why should it happen?

Given the mystery of death, Homo sapiens has been impelled to become a meaning maker. We desperately want our life to make sense. And given our concern about what's to come, we are even willing to give meaning to meaningless activities. Resourceful as we are, we have infinite ways of finding meaning, and infinite potential sources of meaning. In other words, by resorting to innumerable mental acrobatics, we are able to find meaning in every scenario, in every event, in every occurrence, and in every context. Not only do we desire to understand the meaning of life, but even more than that, we want to find out whether our own life could have a deeper meaning. And on top of everything else, we are prepared to do anything but admit that life itself might be meaningless.

Of course, it makes sense to suggest that life will be meaningful only if we give it meaning, leaving it very much up to us. Living the only life we have, we want to make a difference, to make a mark. But it is up to us to make a contribution worth remembering. Doing so will have a positive effect on our sense of self-worth. If we create meaning, we feel much better. But as our sense of self-worth is such a delicate flower, our efforts to create meaning might throw us easily off-balance. We may not find what we are looking for. External events may affect our state of mind. It doesn't take much to cause some form of disequilibrium, to diminish the way we feel about our self. No wonder that our need for meaning making goes into overdrive when something dramatic happens to us—for example, a family tragedy. These situations disturb our sense of self-worth and compel us to question even more deeply why we are here. Many people also experience this disequilibrium when they question their faith. If they repudiate the idea of God and the comforting belief in immortality, what will be left? How will they be able to deal with the void that has been created?

Clearly, what allows us, as human beings, to psychologically survive life on earth, given all its existential challenges, its drama, and its suffering, is finding some form of meaning. For many of us, losing our life may not be the worst thing that can happen. Worse might be losing our reasons for living. For many of us, life is only worth living if we have a specific purpose that inspires us to live.

Defining Meaning and Purpose

Meaning can be redefined as *intent,* or *significance.* It refers to the extent to which we experience life as being directed and motivated by valued goals—in other words, that whatever we are doing matters. We can even see meaning as an experiential byproduct of a life lived in the way we think it should be lived. At the same time, we may also discover that meaning has deeper layers, like the meaning of "meaning," as it may include the intention to communicate something for which we are not consciously aware. There may be some deeper layers that need to be unearthed if we want to find out what's meaningful to us. In this way meaning often turns into a construct and experience shrouded in mystery.

What adds to the confusion about meaning in the anglophone world is that the word *meaning* can have many interpretations in the English language. This is different from many other languages where different words for different aspects of meaning are used. For instance, in Dutch or German there is a clear conceptual difference between *zin* or *sinn* (sense) and *betekenis*/*bedeutung* (meaning), and this opposition plays a central role in all the humanities. Most often, the former denotes the subjective personalized meaning rooted in an individual's life. The latter represents a culturally-defined invariant that can be shared by a common community of language speakers. These differences, however, contribute to the confusion over what we mean by meaning.

In popular use, meaning and purpose tend to be used interchangeably—and often rightly so, when it refers to the worth or value of something. For example, the meaning or purpose of life could refer to the worth or significance of life: my purpose would be to create something meaningful. This interchangeability is not a given, however. For instance, the comment, "there is no meaning in my life" is not the same as "there is no purpose in my life." The differentiation is that meaning is the symbolic value of something while purpose is an objective to be reached, a target, aim, or goal. Thus, to mean something is *to have value, to be definable, to have significance.* To have a purpose, however, means *to bring value* to something, *to make something significant.* In other words, purpose can guide life decisions, influence behavior, shape goals, offer a sense of direction, *and* create meaning. It has a future connotation. In contrast, meaning is the end of purpose. It refers to the past, the present, and the future. Of course, without a sense of purpose, it is hard to find meaning. Also, at times, whatever our purpose is, it may have no meaning at all. We may be engaged in pointless, hollow, empty, futile activities.

But we could also ask ourselves whether our desire to create meaning is inevitable. Is it the curse of being a member of the human race? Is our search for meaning an inevitable outcome of the advanced development of our brain, the by-product of having an inner life? Is it a derivative of our quest for the answer to the Holy Grail of questions, "who am I?"? But whether our search for meaning is a curse or not, it is apparent how our species (even to the point of anguish) looks for meaning in all its activities, whether through the worship of gods, through the application of science, through politics, through business activities, or through art. Homo sapiens find it extremely hard to accept that ultimately anything we do has no meaning. We even go out of our way to create meaning out of seemingly meaningless activities. We find it very difficult to accept that in the end we may be no more than dust in the wind; that all human endeavor and existence amounts to nothing.

Instincts and the Inner World

Although the search for meaning might be the curse of our race, it is also what makes us truly human. Consciousness is unique to humanity. In the animal world, instinctual drives and external stimuli influence behavior. An animal responds immediately to a stimulus that emanates from its direct environment. We can assume that animals do what they do without being concerned with the meaning of life. They might worry about not finding food or a mate but they don't sit around worrying about being enlightened or finding meaning. But for Homo sapiens meaning plays an essential role. Meaning makes us live according to different regulating principles, some of which are inherited from the animal world, and some of which relate to the fact of being distinctly human. It provides us with an inner world that's not merely a picture, or reflection, or image of the outer world.

Thus, to human beings, a meaningless life has none of the dignity of animalistic unselfconsciousness. For us, life cannot simply be reduced to eating, sleeping, foraging, and reproducing. As meaning-seeking creatures, we want much more out of life. It compels us to go beyond simple "here and now" urges and demands. As we have the benefit of an inner world, we want to know who we are; we want to know what's important to us. We want to understand how our external world affects our outlook on life and how our inner theatre affects why we do what we do, so that we may live according to our beliefs and values. The unique personal history each of us has makes our search for meaning an idiosyncratic process. For each of us, it requires a journey into the self. Unlike animals, we are able to relate whatever we think and do to our personal universe. Our actions are determined by the logic within our inner theatre—how the scripts in our inner theatre motivate us to do what we do—these scripts are what makes us unique make us unique.[1]

[1] Joyce McDougall (1991). *Theatres of the Mind.* London: Routledge.

2

In the Shadow of Death

"Don't fear the gods,
Don't worry about death;
What is good is easy to get, and
What is terrible is easy to endure."
—Epicurus

I desire to go to Hell and not to Heaven. In the former I shall enjoy the company of popes, kings and princes, while in the latter are only beggars, monks and apostles.
—Niccolò Machiavelli

Biologically, death can be defined as the permanent cessation of all vital functions. For animals, we imagine that the ending comes as a surprise. But that's not the case for humans. As I have mentioned before, due to the advanced development of our brains, we have the ability to plan ahead. We have the "gift"—if that is the right word to use—of foresight. We can project the future, meaning that we know—difficult as it may be to accept what's going to happen to us—that, eventually, we are going to die. Homo sapiens is burdened with the foresight that we have only a finite stay on earth. And realizing that there will be an ending compels us to search for meaning. In more ways than one, meaning and death can be looked at as two sides of the same coin, a complex interface being the fundamental problem of the human condition.

Unfortunately, the bitter-sweet advantage of foresight brings us to the question of how to face our inevitable death (and the death of people to whom we

M. F. R. Kets de Vries, *Quo Vadis?*, The Palgrave Kets de Vries Library,
https://doi.org/10.1007/978-3-030-66699-6_2

are close) with dignity rather than despair. A number of philosophers have taken a pessimistic view of our ability to do so. Arthur Schopenhauer was one. He wrote: "If the immediate and direct purpose of our life is not suffering then our existence is the most ill-adapted to its purpose in the world: for it is absurd to suppose that the endless affliction of which the world is everywhere full, and which arises out of the need and distress pertaining essentially to life, should be purposeless and purely accidental. Each individual misfortune, to be sure, seems an exceptional occurrence; but misfortune in general is the rule."[1] Clearly, Schopenhauer wasn't a cheerleader. He had a dispiriting view of the human condition. But as he suggests, our attitude towards death will have important implications for our well-being.

What is death? Is it merely the cessation of the biological function of living? Is it the end beyond which there is nothing? Does it imply the disappearance of the soul, the end of consciousness, the evaporation of our personality? Is the disintegration of our body into its elemental components the tragedy to end all tragedies?

As most of us find the disintegration of our body very difficult to imagine, this picture of what is to come prompts the question: is that what life is all about? And if it only ends in death what's the point of living? Others, more hopeful, imagine that there must be a significance, some deep and abiding meaning to death—one that transcends our ability to understand what it's all about.

Whatever our attitude towards death, it is important to talk about it for a very simple reason: whatever stage of life we are at, death hovers like a dark cloud over us, influencing everything we do. Of course, how we experience death varies from person to person. For some, death still remains a distant visitor. For others, death—due to ill health or age—has drawn very close to home. I can recall many instances when a family member or close friend has died. At these times, the riddle of what death is all about becomes personal. It makes me very anxious about the way death cuts me off from people I love and care about. I can no longer look at death as a far-away visitor, removed from my reality. I can no longer distance myself from it. On the contrary, such events force me to face the inevitable. I cannot help but think when it will be my turn. At the same time, it also brings anxiety about the likelihood that other people close to me will die. I ask myself how I will cope when that happens. And of course, like many other people, I have concerns about what will

[1] Arthur Schopenhauer (1981). "On the sufferings of the world," in *The Meaning of Life*, ed. E.D. Klemke, Oxford: Oxford University Press, p. 45.

happen to me after I die—especially since the next step will be into the great unknown. We cannot easily accept the uncertainty of it all.

Death is variously said to detract from life's meaning, to add to life's meaning, or to give life meaning. A wide variety of psychological, spiritual, societal, and cultural meanings have been attached to death. Since the beginning of the history of our species, we always have had great difficulty dealing with the uncertainty of what death brings. To deal with this uncertainty, we have searched for solace in a variety of religions, finding comfort in the belief in an afterlife. Many people console themselves with the idea that they will die but their soul will live on.

Ironically, as a result, many of us imprison ourselves within a wide variety of ritualistic, sometimes even delusional activities. We may resort to totems, taboos, churches, synagogues, temples, and mosques, to push away thoughts of death. We have entered religious wars, prepared to fight to the death to convince the other that our way of looking at life after death is the correct one. In an effort to come to grips with the unacceptable, many of the world's religions provide stark pictures or maps of life after death.

For example, we have Plato's eschatological myth at the end of *The Republic*, the so-called "myth of Er."[2] Here, he addresses one of the greatest philosophical questions of all times: "Where does our soul go when we die and where does it come from when we are born?" It tells the story of Er, a soldier who dies on the battlefield. A number of days later, however, he is returned to life (after having been laid out on his funeral pyre) to report what he experienced in the world beyond. Er talks about the judges who decide which path each soul will follow, depending on the life they led on Earth. The good are told to go to the sky, while the bad are led into the earth. The souls returning from the sky come back clean, telling stories of a place that filled them with good feelings. In contrast, the souls that emerge from the earth are dirty and tell of the misery they faced as punishment for the things that they did while alive. Subsequently, the souls are reborn into a new body and a new life. However, the new life will reflect how they had lived in their previous life and of the state of their soul at death.

Obviously, the tale is a warning that the choices we make and the character we develop will have consequences after our death. The simple moral of the story is that in the afterlife the just will be rewarded and the unjust severely punished—a perspective fitting many religious traditions. Another moral contained within the story might be to try to lead a meaningful life, before death comes to visit.

[2] Plato (2007). *The Republic*. New York: Penguin Classics.

Many religions describe rewards and punishments in the afterlife, depending on our way of living while alive. The *Tibetan Book of the Dead* is a good example of the visualization of after-death experiences. It explains in great depth the Tibetan concept of postmortem existence and is a kind of tourist guide to the afterlife, a funerary text that explains what to expect following death. The text includes innumerable visions of the realms beyond, how to reach eventual liberation, or, failing to do so, how to attain a safe rebirth. According to the text, either we become enlightened, or we will be reborn to experience all over again the sufferings of birth, old age, sickness, and death, stranded in the swamp of cyclic existence.[3]

Another good example of the life to come is the combined artistic imaginations of the poet Dante Alighieri and the early Italian Renaissance painter Sandro Botticelli: the *Inferno* and its humorous but also horrific scenes of torture still retain our fascination today.

In contrast to believers, other people think that death is the end of it all. They suggest that there is no God. They view the concept of God as a desperate outcome of humanity's search for meaning—an attempt to make sense out of the incomprehensible. Or as the existential psychologist Irvin Yalom put it, "Death anxiety is the mother of all religions, which, in one way or another, attempt to temper the anguish of our finitude."[4] For people less attracted to the divine, religion is not perceived as a way to find comfort about death. On the contrary, they suggest that there is nothing behind the curtain of religion apart from what human imagination puts there. Some suggest that atheists are the closest to the truth about living. They are prepared to face reality and will not deceive themselves. They point out that as we don't know where we come from or where we are going, we are driven to fill this void with whatever our imagination can provide. They also imply that resorting to religion is an easy way out of searching for meaning. But they also note that even without belief in a God, it is possible to live a constructive and meaningful life. To quote the evolutionary biologist, Julian Huxley: "But if God and immortality be repudiated, what is left? That is the question usually thrown at the atheist's head. That, however, is because he has only been accustomed to think in terms of his own orthodoxy. In point of fact, a great deal is left… many men and women have led active, or self-sacrificing, or noble, or devoted lives without any belief in God or immortality. Buddhism in its uncorrupted form has no such belief; nor did the great nineteenth-century agnostics; nor do the ortho-

---

[3] https://www.holybooks.com/the-tibetan-book-of-the-dead-2/.

[4] Irvin D. Yalom (2008). *Staring at the Sun: Overcoming the Terror of Death*, San Francisco: Jossey-Bass.

dox Russian Communists; nor did the Stoics. Of course, the unbelievers have often been guilty of selfish or wicked actions; but so have the believers. And in any case that is not the fundamental point. The point is: that without these beliefs men and women may yet possess the mainspring of full and purposive living, and just as strong a sense that existence can be worthwhile as is possible to the most devout believers."[5]

Some atheists are less positive, however. They take a more pessimistic view of life. They argue that if we are just going to die, what is the point of living? Actually, they suggest that the idea of our inevitable death makes living quite absurd. If that really is all there is, shouldn't we just hasten our death? Why should we extend our suffering? For example, to Jean-Paul Sartre, the "absurdity" of human existence is the necessary result of our attempts to live a life of meaning and purpose in an indifferent, uncaring universe. According to him, as there is no God, so there is no perfect and absolute vantage point from which human actions or choices can be said to be rational.[6] That may also be the reason why Albert Camus observed that suicide is the only truly serious philosophical question.[7] Clearly, to Camus life is absurd. Therefore, if our life has no meaning—knowing the suffering that accompanies most people's lives—shouldn't we, instead of waiting for it to happen, just end it? the only act of will. But whatever *Weltanschauung* we subscribe to, each of us, in our own way, should be prepared to explore for ourselves the meaning of our lives in light of our inevitable death.

Tolstoy's Angst

Death and the meaning of life have always figured prominently in the world's literature. For example, they form the theme of the great Russian writer and moralist Leo Tolstoy's famous novella, *The Death of Ivan Ilych*.[8] Tolstoy narrates the story of a worldly careerist, a high court judge who never gave the inevitability of his death a passing thought until death was standing on his doorstep. He describes Ivan Ilych's outlook to life faced with his imminent departure.

In the novella, Tolstoy traces Ivan's life from his birth to his death. According to the story, throughout lvan's life, only superficial and material things

[5] Julian Huxley (2006). *Man in the Modern World*. London: Hesperides Press.

[6] Jean-Paul Sartre (1993). *Being and Nothingness*. New York: Washington Square Press.

[7] Albert Camus (2018). *The Myth of Sisyphus*. New York: Vintage Books.

[8] Leo Tolstoy (2012). *The Death of Ivan Ilych*. New York: Vintage Classics.

mattered to him. Tolstoy not only paints a portrait of a person who is dying, he also helps us understand how we deal with death in our imagination. Ivan Ilych, like many of us, has always been in denial about death and oblivious to the idea of his own mortality.

While Ivan is on his deathbed, he is most troubled by "the deception, the lie, which for some reason they all accepted, that he was not dying but was simply ill, and he only need keep quiet and undergo a treatment and then something very good would result." In particular, the people around him do not admit what they all know and what has dawned on him—that he is dying. In spite of the gravity of his situation, neither the dying man nor the people attending to him are prepared to give their full attention to what's happening. For most of his family and colleagues, Ivan's impending death is an inconvenience—something they would like to put out of their mind. They're relieved—as the living usually are—not to be in Ivan's position, but at the same time, are also perturbed by this reminder of their own mortality. As the anthropologist Margaret Mead put it: "When a person is born we rejoice, and when they're married we jubilate, but when they die, we try to pretend nothing has happened."[9] Tolstoy describes unsparingly the dreadful aloneness of the dying process.

The lies surrounding his deathbed make Ivan more aware of the lies that have been present during his entire life. Before facing death, he had never considered the question of whether the choices he made in his life had been the correct ones. Only now does he realize that he had always been deceiving himself. Only now is he prepared to face the truth that his life had been a living death. Whatever he had done had been motivated by greed and the search for comfort. While ascending through various governmental ranks—earning empty praise from all around him—he had neglected his relationships with his family. His life had been without passion, strong convictions, or value. Now, on his deathbed, Ivan realizes that he doesn't want to die because he has not really lived. Only now, when it is too late, is he prepared to ask himself whether he has wasted the life given to him.

As well as his fatal illness, Ivan is in the grip of a deep spiritual malaise. As death closes in, it dawns on him that he could have lived a very different life: he could have had deep relationships through meaningful human interaction. Instead, his life had been selfish and meaningless. Interestingly, at the point when his life is ending, Ivan seems to undergo a spiritual conversion. As he dies, he realizes the meaninglessness of the life he is leading but seems willing to accept Christ.

---

[9] https://www.quotetab.com/quotes/by-margaret-mead/3.

With Ivan Ilych's story, Tolstoy shows that while everyone dies, not everyone lives. The tragedy of life is what dies inside us while we live. He may have written it to illustrate the meaninglessness of a materialistic outlook on life; that a truly meaningful life is one full of significant relationships. Money will not last. Fame will not last. Power will not last. And our body will not last. But the way we touch others will last.

Tolstoy's complex vision of the afterlife is embodied in his protagonist's ultimate understanding that "instead of death there was light." Thus, although Tolstoy portrays Ivan Ilyich's life as one of petty materialism and illusory exteriors, he suggests that his repentance on his deathbed may redeem him in the eyes of God. (Tolstoy wrote this novella six years after his own radical Christian conversion.) He ends with the hope that when death is close enough, all of us will come to accept and confront it courageously, and with equanimity.

3

A Zen Kōan

How can we know death when we don't know how to live?
—Confucius
I have made a ceaseless effort not to ridicule, not to scorn human actions, but to understand them.
—Baruch Spinoza

The juxtaposition of meaning and death is portrayed well in a famous Zen kōan. Like Tolstoy's novella, it is full of symbolism about how we can live life meaningfully.

> A man traveling in the wilderness encountered a tiger. Terrified, he fled, but the tiger ran after him. At the edge of a cliff, he saw the roots of a wild vine. Grabbing hold of it, he swung himself over the edge, out of the reach of the tiger. The tiger approached the edge of the cliff, roaring at him from above, but unable to reach him. Trembling with fear, the man looked down at the shore below, only to see, to his dismay, another tiger waiting for him to fall. "Could anyone be in a worse position than me?" the traveler asked himself.
>
> Just then, two mice, one black, one white, scampered out of the leaves and began to gnaw away at the roots of the vine. As they chewed and chewed, the man realized his fate. At that moment he saw a juicy strawberry hanging on a ledge next to him. Grasping the vine with one hand, he plucked the strawberry with the other. What a delicious strawberry it was. How sweet it tasted!

There are many different interpretations of this Zen story. Explicitly, it can be seen as a snapshot of the course of our life. How many times do we hear that "death might be just around the corner," that "we should live for the

M. F. R. Kets de Vries, *Quo Vadis?*, The Palgrave Kets de Vries Library,
https://doi.org/10.1007/978-3-030-66699-6_3

moment," that "we should live each day as if it were our last?" The Zen story points out that each moment in space and time is something that we will never, ever experience again. Symbolically, we could view the two tigers as representing our fear of death or suffering, something that the traveler tries to avoid by grasping the roots of the vine. The white and black mice might represent the right or wrong way of dealing with death; they might also represent day and night, indicating that our time on earth is ticking away. The strawberry may symbolize all the good things that life has to offer. Eating the strawberry doesn't just represent an escape from reality—it stands for reality itself. It points out the importance of savoring every day and creating happy moments for ourselves. The vine can represent the timeline of life—hanging between the top of the cliff and the bottom—the latter being death.

It is clear that the traveler's fate is sealed. There can only be one ending: he will be killed by one of the tigers. His death is inevitable, There is no running away so he better accepts what's what coming to him. Like the traveler in this story—not wanting to accept an inescapable fate—many of us do what we can to run from death when its shadow appears before us. We reach for the strawberry –clinging to whatever life-giving alternative is available. In the end, however hard we may try, the mice of mortality will nibble through the vine of life. The only question is how long it will take them to do so. When is it going to happen?

The key message of this story is that life is fleeting and we don't live forever. Each passing moment is gone as fast as it comes. But given the way our lives unfold we would be wise not to fret over what's bound to happen. Our best option is to live in the moment. The present is all we can look forward to. And as death is inescapable, we would be wise not to be totally preoccupied by it. If we do, worry and doubt will poison our present and our future. Reaching out for all the strawberries that come our way is the only way to live a happy, fulfilled life.

As the kōan suggests, it is possible to find moments of happiness even in the most hopeless situation. As long as death hasn't completely nibbled through the vine of life, we should take every bite of life we can. According to the philosopher-emperor Marcus Aurelius, "It is not death that a man should fear, but he should fear never beginning to live." We should really live life to the full. We shouldn't become like Ivan Ilych.

In our journey through life, we are born, and we die. The inescapable fact of our impending death means that we should honor our limited time on earth. We should try to make the best out of it. We should create happy moments. We should keep ourselves centered on the things that give our life meaning. This implies that we should show our deep appreciation for life, that we should explore it to the fullest and value our experiences. To quote the well-known words of Socrates, "The unexamined life is not worth living." Furthermore, we should not forget to express our gratitude for what life has given us.

Tolstoy, in his semi-autobiographical book *A Confession*, presents a parable very like this kōan.[1] Tolstoy's traveler jumps into a dry well to escape a wild beast, only to find a ravenous dragon at the bottom. He saves himself by grabbing a leafy twig that is immediately nibbled by mice, but he notices that there is honey dripping from the leaves and he licks it up. If we don't pick the strawberry or lick up the drops of honey, if we have no more distractions, does life become meaningless? Is the point of life just to create happy moments? Or is there more to it? This question was very much on Tolstoy's mind, when he concluded in *A Confession*: "Faith still remained to me as irrational as it was before, but I could not but admit that it alone gives mankind a reply to the questions of life, and that consequently it makes life possible."[2]

Tolstoy's *A Confession* and *The Death of Ivan Ilych* were written when he was only in his fifties. At that age, he began to think about his forthcoming death. (He lived, however, for another twenty-five years.) It was a point in his life when he became obsessed with the notion of death, having experienced first-hand the horrors of war as a soldier and having had to deal with the death of many members of his family, including five of his children. With his greatest works behind him, he found that his sense of purpose was dwindling. With his celebrity and public acclaim declining, he became depressed, despite having a large estate, good health (for his age), a wife who had borne him fourteen children, and the promise of eternal literary fame. On the brink of suicide, Tolstoy would ask himself whether his life (or any life for that matter) had any meaning. Given the inevitability of death, he wondered whether life was simply absurd.[3] He had been writing to make money, to take care of his family, and to distract himself from his questioning of meaning. But presently—pondering the meaning of life and death—he came to regard his literary work as worthless. He believed that everything he had achieved in life no longer made sense, that it had no purpose. The questions "Why?" "What for?" and "What next?" haunted him incessantly. At first, he imagined that these questions were answerable, but when he found that wasn't the case, Tolstoy began to realize that what he took for a temporary malaise was actually the kind of existential crisis many of us experience: how to face our own death.

[1] Leo Tolstoy (2009). *A Confession.* New York: Merchant Books.

[2] Leo Tolstoy (1983). *A Confession,* New York: W. W. Norton. p. 46.

[3] *Ibid*

Having to face the inevitable made him succumb to a deep spiritual impasse. He wrote:

> "I felt that something had broken within me on which my life had always rested, that I had nothing left to hold on to, and that morally my life had stopped. An invincible force impelled me to get rid of my existence, in one way or another. It cannot be said exactly that I wished to kill myself, for the force which drew me away from life was fuller, more powerful, more general than any mere desire. It was a force like my old aspiration to live, only it impelled me in the opposite direction. It was an aspiration of my whole being to get out of life …
>
> "I did not know what I wanted. I was afraid of life; I was driven to leave it; and in spite of that I still hoped something from it.
>
> "All this took place at a time when so far as all my outer circumstances went, I ought to have been completely happy. I had a good wife who loved me and whom I loved; good children and a large property which was increasing with no pains taken on my part. I was more respected by my kinsfolk …".[4]

In many ways, *A Confession* is the first-person account of Tolstoy's own spiritual journey, from his rejection of religion when he was a young man, through his rediscovery of the Orthodox church in middle age, to his final acceptance of the simple moral teaching of Jesus, ultimately rejecting the pomp and circumstance characteristic of the Orthodox church. But in the end, he found the solution in a kind of irrational knowledge called "faith."

Near Death Experiences

On April 23, 1849, at the age of twenty-eight, the Russian novelist Fyodor Dostoyevsky was arrested for anti-government activities linked to a liberal intellectual group, the Petrashevsky Circle. As the group was suspected of engaging in subversive activities, the tsarist regime sentenced Dostoyevsky to death. Soon after, he was taken to a public square in Saint Petersburg (along with a handful of other inmates) to be shot by firing squad, the execution intended to set an example to the general populace. The prisoners were read their death sentence, put into the white shirts worn by the condemned and allowed to kiss the cross. At that point Dostoyevsky was acutely aware that he had only moments to live. At the last minute, however, the tsar issued a

[4] https://d2y1pz2y630308.cloudfront.net/15471/documents/2016/10/Leo%20Toltstoy-A%20 Confession.pdf; William James (1982). *The Varieties of Religious Experience: A Study in Human Nature*, New York: Penguin Classics, p.122.

pardon. The trial and sentencing had been a cruel publicity stunt to depict the despotic tsar as a benevolent ruler. Dostoyevsky's sentence was commuted to four years of exile with hard labor in Siberia, to be followed by several years of compulsory military service in the tsar's armed forces. He was nearly forty before he was able to resume his literary ambitions.

Having had such a near escape from death, Dostoevsky was full of relief, sensing that he had another chance at life. He noted: "When I look back at the past and think of all the time I squandered in error and idleness, lacking the knowledge I needed to live; when I think of how I sinned against my heart and my soul, then my heart bleeds. Life is a gift, life is happiness … Every minute could have been an eternity of happiness! If youth only knew. Now my life will change, now I will be reborn."[5] By becoming deeply aware of his mortality, he was able to experience life much more intensely. He had acquired a greater sense of purpose that gave meaning to what he did. It put him among the "twice-born," a term describing any experience where there is a strong sense of renewal or rebirth after a dramatic event.[6]

Do we, like Dostoyevsky, find meaning in life because of our impending death? Or is it the other way around? Is it the specter of death that leads us to conclude that our life is meaningless? Near-death experiences can be a catalyst for us to pay renewed attention to the meaning of our life. In Dostoyevsky's case, the dramatic imminence of his death motivated him to become a writer—it compelled him to leave some kind of legacy. It created a life of meaning for him.

Over the course of my life, I've also had a few close calls, incidents that could have changed my life dramatically—or even ended it. I have had a near-death experience on two occasions. The first happened when I was still a student at the University of Amsterdam, very new to the big city. It happened at night, as I left the room where I was boarding, intending to take a streetcar to the center of town. There was a busy intersection with a stop for these busses near where I lived. As I approached the stop, I saw that the streetcar leaving for the city center was ready to leave. I started to sprint to catch it, not watching the oncoming traffic. A second later, I was hit by a car, flying through its window. Panicking, the person driving the car jammed on the brakes with the result that I flew back through the broken window of the car and ended up bleeding miserably and unconscious on the pavement. However, in the short time that I was out, I experienced a strange kind of review—an out-of-body

[5] https://www.goodreads.com/quotes/7789684-when-i-look-back-at-the-past-and-think-of; https://archive.org/stream/lettersoffyodorm00dostiala/lettersoffyodorm00dostiala_djvu.txt.

[6] William James (2018). *The Varieties of Religious Experience: A Study in Human Nature*. New York: Musaicum Books.

experience—of the major scenes of my life. Miraculously, I survived the accident, albeit with some scarring.

My second near-death experience came much later in life. I was visiting Kamchatka, Siberia, one of the wildest regions in the world. At one point, I found myself on a plateau at the top of a mountain. The guide who was with me became highly excited when he saw a bear on the next mountain range and wanted to get closer. Hurrying me to get up behind him on his snowmobile, he set off full speed in the direction of the bear while I tried desperately to hold on and not fall off the snowmobile. Unfortunately, my guide was looking for the bear rather than at what was straight ahead of him. Not paying attention, he drove full speed into a big hole in the snow. He hung on to the machine and didn't have a scratch, but I was thrown off and passed out. I have no idea how long I was unconscious, but I retain a memory of being enveloped in light. When I came to, I was crippled, and in excruciating pain, only to hear my crazy driver saying, "No problem, we have antibiotics!" Later, I discovered that I had broken my spine. Going down the mountain through wet snow with a broken spine was an excruciating exercise in pain management. It felt like torture. Afterwards, it took four operations and many years of recovery to get somewhat back to normal, and for much of that time, I was forced to lie flat. Not a very appealing position for a very active person like me. But I had been lucky, I was told later. I was able to walk again.

People who report on near-death experiences mention a variety of sensations, including detachment from the body, feelings of levitation, a feeling of serenity, security, or warmth, the sense of absolute dissolution, the presence of a light, and experiencing a life review. In my case, in my first accident, I experienced a kind of life review, commonly referred to as "seeing your life flash before your eyes." From the second accident, I recall only the presence of a great light. Of course, I could attribute these visions and apparitions to the neurochemicals in my brain working overtime in response to trauma; our brains may do some interesting things just before we die.

Near-death experiences can be transformational. People who live through them usually report a greater appreciation for life, a greater sense of purpose and self-understanding, more compassion for others, fewer concerns about material wealth, a desire to learn, elevated spirituality, a feeling of being more intuitive, greater ecological sensitivity—and an overall feeling of personal strength. A small percentage of people, however, report feelings of fear, depression, and obsessional thoughts about death. Others have heightened religious sensations and emerge with convictions about a spiritual world. Some survivors of these experiences emerge with no fear of death and in fact assume that a positive experience will await them when they do actually die.[7]

Personally, all I can say is that these experiences made me more appreciative of life. They also helped me to acquire a greater sense of purpose in everything I do. I believe they may have made me more empathetic and less judgmental, and generally more effective as a helping professional.

Death can turn into a deadline with serious implications if we haven't done what we set out to do and deadlines often motivate us to take the actions needed to achieve what we want to achieve. Taking my own experience as an example, the imminence of death can reveal that human life is very fragile and, in turn, prompt a greater appreciation of life. This begs the question of the concept of immortality: if we could live forever, would we recognize what a gift life is? Without the death deadline, would we experience the same urgency to find our own, unique way to live meaningfully? It seems that death and meaning are inseparable partners in the dance of life.

The Book of Revelation

The premise of the greatest work by Ingmar Bergman, his famous allegorical film "The Seventh Seal" is stark: a knight and his squire return from the Crusades to find Sweden in a state of anarchy.[8] The country is convulsed by witch hunts and religious mania, while Europe is suffering from the bubonic plague, which caused the death of a third of its population.

In the film, Death confronts the knight and tells him that his time is up. In response, in a desperate but futile attempt to prolong his life, the knight challenges Death to a chess game with his life as the prize. Although death is all around, the knight tries to avoid the fact that it is his turn to die. His behavior inspires Death to ask, "How can you outwit Death?" Although the knight understands that it is absurd to try to, he is nonetheless compelled to cheat by trying to checkmate Death. The outcome is predictable. The film ends with a *danse macabre*, with Death summoning representatives from all walks of life to dance along to the grave, one of the most iconic cinematic images of all

[7] George Gallup and William Proctor (1984). *Adventures in Immortality: A Look Beyond the Threshold of Death.* London: Corgi; Kenneth Ring (1984). *Heading toward Omega. In search of the Meaning of Near-Death Experience.* New York: William Morrow.

[8] The title of the film refers to a passage about the end of the world from the *Book of Revelation*, used both at the very start and the end of the film: "And when the Lamb had opened the seventh seal, there was silence in heaven about the space of half an hour."

time. As Death says in the film, “No one escapes me,” regardless of station or rank.

Our awareness of our mortality will motivate some of us, and demotivate others. And confusingly, the sense of mortality can simultaneously motivate and demotivate the same person. How our dance with death will turn out depends on our inner theatre—our major inner drivers—and our reactions to our external circumstances. We need to pay attention to our unconscious and work out what kind of “stealth motivator” death will be for each of us, how death will influence our conscious and unconscious thought processes, and how it will influence our actions.[9]

Many of us come to realize that life is very short and that, during our short stay on earth, death is our constant companion. We cannot escape this deathwatch, or the feeling of nothingness that may accompany thoughts about the end of our existence. At the same time, the inevitability of death will give our life meaning—but only if we want it to. This makes death both a destroyer and a sense-maker. But do we really need a near-death experience to be able to arrive at meaning-making? Or are there other ways to go about it?

[9] Manfred F. R. Kets de Vries (2014). Death and the executive: encounters with the “stealth motivator,” *Organizational Dynamics*, 43 (4), pp. 247–256

4

Death as Meaning-Maker

Life and death are important. Don't suffer them in vain.
—Bodhidharma
That it will never come again is what makes life so sweet.
—Emily Dickinson

Our first breath is the beginning of our journey towards death, and as a consequence we consider death the enemy. But is that the right attitude to take? Doesn't being alive become more precious precisely because of our inevitable death? Doesn't death teach us the value of time? Doesn't death create "deadlines" that motivate us to get the most out of life?

In many ways, death is a medicine that helps us feel more alive. And when we realize its significance, consciously or unconsciously, we're more likely to spend our time wisely. But although this may be a truism, there are many people who are apparently unaware of death's reality. They don't seem to appreciate the value of time. All too often, they busy themselves doing the kinds of things that don't matter very much, not wanting to recognize that death is hovering about. Instead, they take flight in the "manic defense," the tendency some have, when presented with uncomfortable thoughts or feelings, to distract the conscious mind with a flurry of trivial activities.[1]

[1] Manfred F. R. Kets de Vries (2020). *The CEO Whisperer: Meditation on Leaders, Life and Change*, in press.

M. F. R. Kets de Vries, *Quo Vadis?*, The Palgrave Kets de Vries Library,
https://doi.org/10.1007/978-3-030-66699-6_4

One of my clients described this behavior pattern to me and her sense that she was running away from something. She described feeling compelled to work constantly, whether what she did was important or not. She needed always to be busy, to distract herself. "It's like I have to tire myself out. If not, I get too many gloomy thoughts." She worked very long hours then pretty much forced the people she worked with to join her for dinners or go to discos. "It's another way of distracting myself. It's like I have to create a lot of external noise to drown out the inner demons." Having recognized what was driving her behavior, she started to question whether she made any meaningful "noise," and admitted that she had problems forming relationships. "It's not that people don't try. Plenty of men show an interest in me but I see them more like accessories, something else I can distract myself with. I've never had a meaningful relationship with anyone." She talked about the "emptiness inside" that never seemed to go away.

The behavior of my client resembles that of Ivan Ilych. Subliminally, although aware that she was keeping herself busy with meaningless activities, she preferred not to see. Although people like my client might recognize this kind of mindless behavior pattern in others, they don't want to see it in themselves. They prefer to hang on to the delusion that they are different. A number of them, although pretending to be interested in the pursuit of meaning, are in reality only interested in wealth, power, status, and sex. What they don't realize is that conscious living can only truly begin when they understand what brings enduring meaning. To put it neatly, finding meaning is what makes the difference between making a living and making a life.

Remember Ted in Chap. 1? His initial response to his existential crisis (and quite a common reaction) was similarly to resort to this "manic defense." "Busyness" was his habitual defensive mode. Pushing away thoughts of death through the flight into action can be an attractive option. In Ted's case, it also provided him with the means of making a living, but he was also using this frenzy of activities to chase away his demons. Nevertheless, the fact that Ted had started to doubt his own existence was proof that he had a mind of his own, that there was someone inside him who was very much alive.

Ted's strategy had served him well for some time, despite his deteriorating marriage and his loss of interest in his work, but as he learned the hard way it wasn't completely fool proof. Eventually, his lack of purpose and loneliness brought matters to a head, leading him to question the point of his existence.

Ted was forced to face life's transience. When his defensive maneuvers let him down, he had to accept that death is an immovable object that cannot be pushed away. There were more and more reminders of this as people close to him fell ill and died. Having come to realize that we are all born into this world alone and will leave it alone, how he could deal better with the interval? Deep down, Ted's existential crisis was a signal that he needed to do something more significant with his life, and to have more meaningful relationships.

Ted's story can be taken as a cautionary tale, suggesting that the extent to which we deal well with life depends on how we face the fact of death on our life's journey. Facing death on our deathbed—like Ivan Ilych—isn't really the way to go. To be born again, with our last breath, is not really the answer. When we reach this point in our life, when it's too late to do anything about it, we are more likely to suffer from serious remorse for not having lived life to its fullest. Unfortunately, too many people resemble Ivan Ilych and turn desperately to religion in an attempt to find salvation. The question is whether they shouldn't have prepared for this transition at a much earlier stage of life. The philosopher Voltaire had no truck with this. When asked by a priest on his deathbed to renounce the devil and to commit his soul to God, he replied, "Now, now, good man, this is no time to make new enemies."

Some people see death as the next great adventure. Others, like Ivan Ilych, are afraid of dying because they haven't yet lived. Still others take their impending death with equanimity, seeing it as the end of it all—but believing that they have lived a rich, fulfilling life. They are prepared to accept whatever is coming their way.

La Petite Mort

Other people—perhaps more fatalistic or happy-go-lucky than Ted—accept the fact that death is inescapable but wonder why they should bother engaging in meaningful activities. Why not simply coast through life? Why not live for the moment, pick the strawberry, lick the honey? Their response to the narcissistic injury of non-existence is hedonistic—sex and drugs and rock and roll. Instead of the busyness of work they opt for another kind of busyness. *Carpe deum*—seize the day—forget all this business of meaning, leave that to philosophers. There's something to be said for this choice—better than narcissistic gloom, manic busyness, or anxiety attacks. But how satisfying is it in the long run?

For other people, the anti-depressant of choice is sex. The French talk about *la petite mort*, which means "a little death," referring to orgasm, and probably derived from the Greco-Roman belief that each orgasm saps away a little bit of life. In my work, I have met a number people addicted to *la petite mort*, through which they try to exorcise *la grande mort*, death itself. Sex is their way to prove that they are still alive. Of course, with each orgasm comes the possibility of pregnancy, so ironically, "the little death" can also be the beginning of life.

Death and the Life Cycle

La petite mort aside, death imagery tends to preoccupy us from an early age, consciously or unconsciously. Throughout our life, we are always subliminally aware of death, but our attitude towards it changes as we age. For example, at five to seven, most children understand that death is irreversible, that it ends all life functions, and that it is something that will also happen to them. Often, the death of pets gives children an inkling of what's to come. But death becomes more real when they learn of the death of a close relative or family friend and realize that people close to them, especially their parents, are not immortal. This somber discovery leads them to question of how they will be able to cope with the loss of the people they love and depend on. How will they look after themselves when they are no longer there? When children come to this realization, the world they originally believed to be permanent is turned upside down.

Although it happened many decades ago, I still remember quite starkly the first dramatic death I experienced. It was the death of my grandmother from pneumonia, at a relatively early age. (I describe this in my book *Sex, Money, Happiness and Death*).[2] I have an eidetic memory of my grandmother bathing me in the kitchen while she sang songs to me that I still remember. (She used to play in an amateur operetta ensemble.) From time to time, as if she had a premonition that she wouldn't live long, she would ask me if I would remember her when she was gone. The question—which, looking back, was rather unfair—was beyond me as I was only five years old. I didn't know how to react to it. Of course, I thought she would always be there. To me, her death was unimaginable. I didn't want to think about, let alone deal with it. But when it happened, seeing her laid out in her coffin in the "nice" room of the old farmhouse where they lived, something changed in me. My world would never be the same. Death had entered my imagination. But I soon learned that I also needed to get on with life. My grandmother haunted my thoughts, however. As a key force in the family, her death had a huge effect on the overall family dynamics.

---

[2] Manfred F. R. Kets de Vries (2009). *Sex, Money, Happiness, and Death: The Quest for Authenticity*. New York: Palgrave Macmillan.

As a psychoanalyst, I have been privy to a number of cases where children have recurring nightmares and trouble sleeping induced by the fear of being left behind. They are afraid there will be no parents to take care of them. But regardless of when this discovery of impermanence occurs, it effectively destroys a child's narcissistic feeling of omnipotence. Instead, it creates a feeling of vulnerability—a realization that nothing lasts forever. And even though their defenses come to the rescue and block death awareness from consciousness, these fears are preserved intact in their unconscious. Thereafter, the repressed fear of death continues to exert a significant influence on the development of the child, and later, as an adult.

Adolescents fully understand the meaning of death, but often believe that they are somehow immortal. As a result, they may engage in risky behavior, such as driving recklessly, using drugs, drinking or smoking to excess, with little thought of the perilous consequences. It is during the years of young adulthood (20–40), however, that death anxiety begins to become more prevalent. The forces of denial become less effective. Most young and middle-aged adults will have gained a more realistic view of death, as it is quite likely, at this stage, that they have experienced the death of a number of close family members or friends. And as we continue to age, most of us arrive at greater acceptance that our loved ones will die. What's more, the inevitability of this makes us more accepting of our own death.

When we enter later adulthood, many of us, having a greater sense of tranquility (if we believe that we are living a meaningful life), come to accept the inevitability of our own demise. However, during the next phase of life (40–64), death anxiety seems to peak at its highest level compared to other stages of our life. This is understandable as, by this phase of life, we increasingly face our own physical decline and are grieving the death of our parents. Also, at this later stage of life—with the notion of death ever-present—we start to live more day by day. We become more cognizant of the need to make the most of whatever time we have left. Surprisingly, levels of death anxiety slump off once we are 65 and more.[3] But it isn't a given. If they don't think that they have lived a meaningful life, older people may react to their impending death with feelings of regret, bitterness, or even despair.

[3] Megan Trenner (1982). Accuracy of perception and attitude: An intergenerational investigation, *Perceptual and Motor Skills*. 54 (1), pp. 271–274.

An Uncertain Expiration Date

What you would do if you had only an hour left to live? What about just one day? Only a month? A year? Keeping your responses in mind, what would you do the rest of your life?

The purpose of this exercise is to underline that you shouldn't take your life for granted. Urgency helps you focus on the things that really matter. You could now ask yourself what effect the uncertainty of not knowing when you will die has on you. Would your life be more meaningful if its endpoint was known rather than unknown? Would having a definite expiration date make you more inclined to pursue meaning?

Death is both inevitable and uncertain. We know it will happen, but we don't know when. When I ask people at what age they think that they will die, many have great difficulty in responding. Obviously, it is not the kind of question people like to deal with. Some don't want to think about it at all and become quite evasive. Others come up with a date or age, usually based on the death of their own parents or someone else important to them. We tend to become preoccupied with death when we approach the age at which one of our parents died. This "anniversary reaction" prompts unsettling feelings, thoughts, or memories. Others, however, prefer to park this question, as if they hope that science will eventually conquer death or, at least, postpone it for a very long time. These are the kinds of people who busily search out rejuvenation techniques, such as cosmetic surgery, implantation of stem cells, and homeopathic treatments. The cynic in me tends to think that the same people who long for immortality are those who have no idea what to do with themselves when stuck at home on a snowy day.

In Chap. 3, we saw the effect an expected expiration date had on Dostoyevsky. The likelihood of losing his life made him realize its true value. It motivated him to make the most of it. Wouldn't all of us be better off if we had some kind of near-death experience during our lifetime? Wouldn't we put greater value on our limited time on earth? Knowing our expiration date will make procrastination less of an issue. We would be less likely to squander whatever opportunities remain open to us.

Death remains a mystery to all of us. What is absolutely certain, however, is that we will die, but we don't know when or how. We usually seize on this as an excuse to postpone dealing with death head on. However, when we know that death is near, everything else snaps into perspective. Our imminent death focuses the mind and can be a great motivator to try to make our life more meaningful. It may compel us to reprioritize and accomplish certain goals. And perhaps knowing the exact date of our death would make us more likely to turn away status- or achievement-oriented goals like wealth, power and fame. We might choose more meaningful goals, such as close personal relationships and/or devoting ourselves to making the world a better place.

Having a definite "expiration date" could be a transformational experience. An example of this was Randy Pausch, a computer science professor at Carnegie Mellon University, who was diagnosed with pancreatic cancer and told that he had only months to live (he died at the age of 47). Ironically, it was a tradition at his university to ask professors to imagine that they were dying, supposedly as a way to get them to talk about what mattered most to them during their life. Unlike the others, however, this question was brutal reality for Pausch. Knowing that his end was near, he gave his "last lecture," telling the audience how the awareness of death can motivate a person, and even play a major role in enhancing the meaning of someone's life. In his lecture, Pausch spoke about the relevance of achieving childhood dreams as well as the lessons he had learned in life. He mentioned the importance of overcoming obstacles, of enabling the dreams of others, of seizing every moment (because time is all you have). Also, he referred to the importance of having fun in life: "You just have to decide if you're a Tigger or an Eeyore. I think I'm clear where I stand on the great Tigger/Eeyore debate. Never lose the childlike wonder."[4] Obviously, having a positive attitude toward life had always been a key characteristic for Pausch.

This touching lecture was viewed more than 17 million times on the Internet and a book based on his lecture (which Pausch co-authored) sold more than five million copies. Pausch showed people how to make the best of their ending. Clearly, when people learn that they will die soon—for example, on receiving a diagnosis of a terminal disease—reflection on their impending death may motivate them to make the most of their remaining days. Sadly enough, however, in many cases, their disease prevents them from doing so.

Eugene O'Kelly's book, *Chasing Daylight*, describes how to embrace death without fear or sadness.[5] O'Kelly had been the CEO and Chairman of KPMG in the United States until he was diagnosed with a terminal brain tumor at the age of 53. He quit his job to settle his accounts with friends and family and wrote a book (the final chapter was written by his wife) to convey how he lived his last hundred days and (according to him) made it the best time of his life. To those considering taking the time someday to plan their final weeks

[4] Randy Pausch (2008). *The Last Lecture: Really Achieving Your Childhood Dreams - Lessons in Living*. Kindle Edition.

[5] Eugene O'Kelly (2007). *Chasing Daylight: How My Forthcoming Death Transformed My Life*. New York: McGraw Hill.

and months, he counseled "Move it up." During the last period of his life, O'Kelly seemed to have discovered the world he was living in, in a way he had never done before: nature, connections with people close to him, and living in the moment. Also, his religious faith was a great help to him in facing his final days.

Toward the end of his life, the great American entrepreneur, Steve Jobs, said, "Remembering that I'll be dead soon is the most important tool I've ever encountered to help me make the big choices in life." The experiences of these three men suggest that, paradoxically, death can hold the key to living a vital and meaningful life. What may turn out to be the most effective way to protect ourselves from the terror of death is to actively pursue a meaningful life, despite the shadow death casts over us.

Perhaps it's time to ask yourself what *your* last lecture would be like? What are the lessons that you have learned in your life? If you knew how much time you had left, what would you change in the way you live your life now?

5

Death Anxiety

To fear death is nothing other than to think oneself wise when one is not. For it is to think one knows what one does not know. No one knows whether death may not even turn out to be the greatest blessings of human beings. And yet people fear it as if they knew for certain it is the greatest evil.

—Socrates

Death, the only immortal who treats us all alike, whose pity and whose peace and whose refuge are for all—the soiled and the pure, the rich and the poor, the loved and the unloved.

—Mark Twain

Humans are unique in that they must learn to live and adapt to the consciousness of their own finiteness. Human behavior has always been influenced by the specter of death and life's impermanence. Throughout recorded history, awareness of our mortality and the fear of death have been universal psychological quandaries for the human race. For many people, death is a black abyss, the end of all experience. It connotes a sense of nothingness, the total extinction of being. That fear is fed by the dread of what (something? nothing?) might come next and the loss of everything we have ever valued. Whatever we have accomplished—whatever our material riches may be—we cannot take it with us. There is the dread of losing control of the things and people we are responsible for—particularly the ability to protect our dependents. There is also the fear of the pain and loneliness of dying or suffering a violent or painful death. For some, there is also the fear of failing to complete

M. F. R. Kets de Vries, *Quo Vadis?*, The Palgrave Kets de Vries Library,
https://doi.org/10.1007/978-3-030-66699-6_5

their life's work. For many artists and scientists, the fear of death stems from anxiety at not being able to complete their mission or calling in life.

Given all these concerns, it is no surprise that death anxiety—the threat of non-being—has been Homo sapiens' constant companion. It shadows us in whatever we do and wherever we go. We would prefer to die in our sleep, without pain and without awareness. Dying well, however, must start with death acceptance—finishing whatever needs to be done; feeling a sense of pride in our achievements; setting things right with family and friends; and making peace with the inevitable. Actually, dying well could be hard work, because dying is more than a mere physical process. It is a process that includes our whole being—physical, psychological, and spiritual.

My father lived to be 101, plus some months. At that point in his life he decided that he had had enough. For many years, having always led a very active life as the president of a company, he had felt (even though he never expressed it directly) that the quality of his life was no longer what he wanted. As the years passed, his physical condition gradually deteriorated, until he could do very little of substance. Almost everyone in his generation had died. His brothers and sisters had died a long time ago. And although people in the next generations, in particular his children and grandchildren, visited him regularly, not having the old familiar faces around created a sense of loneliness. He became very dependent on a number of caregivers—a difficult proposition for a man who had always been in control of his life. But as things were, at the dusk of his life, he rarely left his house. Due his physical condition, only a few things gave him pleasure. Thus, given his dissatisfaction with his lifestyle, he made the decision that the time has come for him to die. In many ways, he was very fortunate not to live in an old people's home or to have to be hospitalized. Instead, he was very well taken care of in his own house. Like most of us, he wanted to die at home.

After my father had made his decision, he asked his four children to come to his house, telling us that he thought his time was up. Subsequently, in spite of all our protestations—all of us finding it very hard to imagine life without him—he stopped eating and drinking. A few days later he died in my arms. The ending was a strange but magical experience but also a way I wouldn't mind going into that "good night."

Did my father live a full life? Did he live a life of meaning? My answer to these questions is affirmative, in particular, given all the things he did during World War II, when he saved the lives of many people. Could he have done certain things differently? Could he have made different choices? Absolutely, but I always imagined that he did the best he could, given the circumstances. After all, we are all only human. It is fine to be "good enough."

At the time, my father's death reminded me once more of what's coming. Again, it brought home to me to the questions of why we are here, of what's the meaning of life. Our ability to entertain these kinds of reflections is what differentiates us from the other creatures in the animal kingdom. We want to find reasons why death is part of our life's journey. We want to know why we're here. No wonder that concerns about mortality have featured heavily in both ancient and modern art, literature, theater, philosophy, and psychology, indicating that death anxiety is humankind's most basic fear. Because it is a specific characteristic of our species, it greatly affects our outlook on the world. For as long as human beings have been recording their history, the anxiety about what's to come has been a pervasive theme.[1]

Just looking around us we can see that death—in spite of our formidable defense of denial—has always held great symbolic meaning for us all, the presence of so many complex funeral practices being important signifiers. In cultures worldwide, evidence of burial rites has been found dating back more than 100,000 years. Through time, mounds of earth, temples, pyramids, cists, and underground caverns have been uncovered, shedding light on the customs of our predecessors, from Egyptian mummification practices, to bodies preserved in peat bogs, to dead Vikings sent out in burning ships-turned-crematoriums, to sky burials, with human corpses placed on mountaintops to be eaten by carrion birds.

How we view death and how we cope with death anxiety profoundly affects every aspect of our lives—either positively or negatively. We can even argue that all human drama is, to a great extent, a story of how we, as human beings, cope with the terror of death—how we try to overcome death anxiety—how we resort to a great variety of conscious efforts and unconscious defense mechanisms.[2] But, as I mentioned before, in spite of all our defenses, our anxiety about our mortality (often triggered by events like losing a loved one, hearing about a tragedy, or experiencing a health scare) may have an existential purpose. It is a reminder that we need to make the most of the life we have; that meaning can be the antidote to death anxiety.

[1] Elizabeth Kübler-Ross (1969). *On Death and Dying.* New York: Macmillan; Greg Palmer (1993), *Death: The Trip of a Lifetime.* San Francisco: Harper.

[2] Robert Kastenbaum (2000). *The Psychology of Death* (3rd ed.). New York: Springer.

The Mother of All Concerns

All human existence is embedded in time—past, present, future—therefore, given our ability to look forward, we have to face the specter of death. But apprehension about our forthcoming death is a normal part of the human condition. In this context we have predatory death anxiety, the most basic and oldest form of death anxiety, which arises from the fear of being harmed due to an external threat. After all, the main purpose of life is to stay alive. To observe the impact of predatory anxiety, we need only watch animal behavior. All animals make incredible efforts to stay alive.[3] They don't want to be harmed; they don't want to be eaten. If a lion chases a zebra, it tries to escape—and so will we, when a lion comes at us.

I remember sitting at a small spring in the wilds of Zimbabwe, an ideal spot to watch wildlife. I was very well-camouflaged, partially covered by rocks, and hidden by some thorn bushes. I was looking out for the kudus that regularly visited the spring. At dusk, I saw some movement. When I looked closer, I realized it was not the kind of movement I had expected. What I saw was a lioness who also must have been a regular visitor to this spring. I still remember the gleam in her eyes when she glanced at me. She stopped, came closer, looked at me once more, and moved off. The lioness let it go. But like any zebra, I recognized that this animal could have been a direct threat to my life. I had an intense adrenaline rush. At the time, I felt very much like a wild animal, in fear for my life. But zebras, unlike human beings, don't sit in the safety of an office preoccupied by the fact that they will eventually die. Human animals are preyed on by these kinds of thoughts; zebras only know they are prey when something armed with teeth and claws comes after them.

The question becomes, how do we cope with this fear of death? What do we do to make it manageable? Some people will be more accepting of what's to come while others will experience overwhelming anxiety when thinking about their own death or about the process of dying. To these people, the death anxiety can turn into an obsession. Understandably, death anxiety turns out to be a basic fear underlying various psychological conditions. And although it is considered natural to experience a degree of anxiety about our own death, when it turns into a persistent, haunting fear that interferes with our daily activities, we may be suffering from thanatophobia.

[3] Emanuele Castano, Bernard Leidner, Alain Bonacossa, John Nikkah, Rachel Perrulli, Bettina Spencer and Nicholas Humphrey (2011), Ideology, fear of death, and death anxiety, *Political Psychology*, 32 (4), pp. 601–621.

In the Greek language, the word "thanatos" refers to death and "phobos" means fear. Thus, thanatophobia can be translated as a fear of death or a fear of the dying process. In Greek mythology, Thanatos was the god of death. Interestingly enough, he was said to be the twin brother of Hypnos, the god of sleep, which is sometimes described as death's little brother. And deep, dreamless sleep—the total cessation of consciousness—is how many of us imagine death is going to be like. The description of sleep as "the little death" (very much like "la petite mort") is based on the belief that every night our spirits travel to the spirit world while we sleep, the land of the dead, also known as the dream world, a journey that recharges us.

Death takes the form of mythical figures in many cultures. For example, in the Hindu pantheon, there is Yama, the god of death. He is portrayed as very frightening apparition, with four arms, protruding fangs, and a wrathful expression. He is surrounded by flames, and holds a noose and a mace or sword, riding a water-buffalo. The noose is used to grab people who are about to die. In the Netherlands (and to a lesser extent in Belgium) the personification of Death is "*Magere Hein*" ("*Meager Hein*"). The concept of Magere Hein originally came from pagan beliefs but seems to have made an appearance in the Middle Ages. Magere Hein is dressed as a skeleton with a black robe, and a scythe, the latter used to cut people's life cord. It was influenced by the *Dance macabre* (Dance of Death), the prevalent imagery of death at that time.

Many of the people who suffer from thanatophobia lose their *joie de vivre*—their lust for life. Although the condition has not been defined as a distinct disorder, it is often linked to depression and anxiety disorders such as post-traumatic stress, panic disorders, and hypochondriasis. Thanatophobia may also be expressed as a fear of separation, the fear of loss, and/or worry about leaving loved ones behind, and fear about all the bad things that can happen to a person.

All of us, to some extent, suffer from death anxiety. For people suffering from thanatophobia, however, the fear of dying has turned into a terrifying companion. They have great difficulty dealing with the idea of their death. As a result, their fears center on anything that can be associated with death, such as contamination by germs, dangerous objects, risky situations, or people who are perceived as harmful. And as is to be expected, if these fears are present on a permanent basis, they will get in the way of everyday life. In its most extreme manifestation, these feelings can stop people from conducting their daily activities to the point of being afraid to leave their homes. Paradoxically, it is exactly this fear of death that may prove to be deadly. People suffering from thanatophobia may devise bizarre, meaningless ways to protect their life, activities that could destroy them. To illustrate, we could take as extreme example of thanatophobia Howard Hughes, the business magnate, investor, record-setting pilot and film director, known during his lifetime as one of the most financially successful individuals in the world. Later in life, his death anxiety became expressed as a phobia about germs. It motivated him to adopt increasingly bizarre rituals. Hughes insisted on using tissues to pick up objects to insulate himself from germs. He would notice dust, stains, or other imperfections on people's clothes and demand that they take care of them. Eventually, his behavior became so extreme that at the end of his life, he spent most of his time fixated in his chair, often naked, continually watching movies, neither bathing nor cutting his hair and nails. When he died—given his strange lifestyle—he was practically unrecognizable. His tall frame barely weighed ninety pounds.

Many psychological and physical symptoms can be traced back to death anxiety. For example, death anxiety might explain why some people are ambivalent about having children, due to obsessional thoughts that they will die. Death anxiety can also be the reason for many unnecessary health procedures, if people are fearful of contracting a deadly illness. Hypochondriacal preoccupations come into this category. The origin of many phobic reactions is also death anxiety. People suffering from excessive death anxiety may also suffer from sleep disorders, as they may be haunted by thoughts of death during the night. For example, I remember someone once telling me, "I've always been scared to death of pain—afraid, even, to think about it. But whatever I do to push these thoughts away, they come back to me in my dreams."

Others, due to their constant thinking about death, experience feelings of powerlessness, loneliness, loss of control, and meaninglessness, preventing any peace of mind. And as is to be expected, their preoccupation with death will also negatively impact these sufferers' ways of thinking and decision-making capabilities, leaving them susceptible to intense emotions and impulsive, irrational reactions. The long and the short of it is that the awareness of our finite existence (be it a conscious or unconscious process), can have a profound impact on all our emotions, thoughts, and behavior. The intensity of this experience will fluctuate, however, depending on a person's feeling of inner security. Thanatophobic people are at the extreme end of the scale. Generally speaking, death anxiety will have less impact on people who have a secure sense of self-esteem, suggesting that possessing a solid sense of self-esteem is connected to meaningful activity.[4]

[4]Victoria L. Buzzanga, Holly R. Miller, Sharon E. Perne, Julie A. Sander, and Stephen F. Davis (1989). The relationship between death anxiety and level of self-esteem: A reassessment, *Bulletin of the Psychonomic Society*, 27 (6), pp. *570–572.*

Ironically, when I ask people how thoughts of death influence their behavior, many respond flippantly that they rarely think about death. But, as I noted earlier, they are ignoring the influence of their unconscious and the power of their psychological defenses. At an unconscious level, cognizance of their eventual demise will be ever-present. Although it may be unwittingly, all of us are prone to death anxiety, feelings that will influence significant aspects of our lives. And as I have suggested repeatedly, death anxiety is the driver behind our search for meaning and will motivate many of our actions. In that respect, death can be seen as a stealth motivator.[5] And once more, this signifies that meaning and death are two sides of the same coin.

Various studies show that many of the people who want to hasten their death by committing suicide, or who ask for euthanasia in countries where it is permitted, are not motivated—as we might assume—by the experience of being in physical pain. Many of them reported feelings of depression, hopelessness, and meaninglessness.[6] The main reason people asked for assisted suicide was because they had lost any sense of meaning in their lives.

Much of what drives us to do what we do derives from our attempts to keep death anxiety at bay or to defeat death, at least symbolically. And we resort to a large number of defensive maneuvers to ward off death's threatening imagery. However, in spite of all our efforts to the contrary, our preoccupation with death will seep into our consciousness, demonstrating the limited success of our defensive strategies and affecting our motivation in whatever we do.

The Salient Role of Denial

Among our many maneuvers to evade thoughts of death, denial is our major defense against death-related thoughts. We prefer not to think of these frightening realities rather than face our fears head-on. But not thinking about death will not make life last forever. The ancient tale of Death in Samarra makes this message clear.

> A long, long time ago, a merchant in Baghdad sent his servant to the marketplace for provisions. Soon afterwards, the servant came running home white as a sheet. Trembling with fear, he told the merchant: "Master, just now I was in the marketplace, jostled by a woman in the crowd. When I looked closer, I realized that it was Death who made a threatening gesture at me."

---

[5] Manfred F. R. Kets de Vries (2014). Death and the executive: Encounters with the "stealth motivator," *Organizational Dynamics*, 43 (4), pp. 247–256.

[6] William Breitbart (2014). *Psychosocial Palliative Care.* New York: Oxford University Press.

> Panic-stricken, the servant asked the merchant to lend him his fastest horse to flee to Samarra, a town more than hundred kilometers away where he believed Death would not be able to find him.
>
> Sometime later, annoyed but curious, the merchant walked to the marketplace and found Death. He asked her why she had threatened his servant that morning. She replied, "I didn't mean to frighten him, but I was so surprised. I was astonished to see him in Baghdad because I have an appointment with him tonight in Samarra."

Like the servant in this tale, we try to run away from death. Western society, in particular, is very skilled at denial. Quite often, in conversations, death is the elephant in the room. We like to behave as if is is not present. We tend to live in death-phobic cultures. Compared to other regions of the world, we are much more reluctant to deal with the idea of our forthcoming death, cosmetic surgery, special diets, and exercise programs being popular choices to maintain the illusion of youth. The existential psychologist Irvin Yalom puts this attitude in perspective when he notes that dealing with death anxiety is like staring at the sun. We can only look at it for a few seconds before we experience the need to turn away.[7] Or to quote the French writer François de la Rochefoucauld, "Neither the sun nor death can be looked at with a steady eye." Far too quickly, when the idea of death comes to consciousness, our defenses start to work overtime. We prefer to keep death out of sight and out of mind, leaving its unpleasant details to hospitals and funeral parlors.

While the defense mechanism of denial can be adaptive in limited doses, its excessive use can become emotionally very costly. Denying the presence of death doesn't enrich either the preciousness of each moment or our detachment from it. Although we may not realize it, denial comes to the fore through a wide range of mental mechanisms and physical actions, many of which go unrecognized as they tend to take place at an unconscious level. For example, denial seems to be at the root of such diverse actions as breaking the rules, violating frames and boundaries, manic celebrations, violence toward others, and other forms of unethical behavior. I have also observed how people in the grip of death anxiety can become increasingly defensive in ways that can be harmful to themselves and often to others. But while they are trying to protect themselves from the fear of death through denial, they may lose the perspective of what's important in life. They may give importance to insignificant issues while failing to value other relevant and more meaningful activities.

---

[7] Irvin D. Yalom (2008). *Staring at the Sun: Overcoming the Terror of Death,* San Francisco: Jossey-Bass.

Some of them even live their lives pretending that they will never die. They go through life as if they can afford to squander whatever time they have left. But in their manic efforts to keep death at bay, they risk diminishing their possible range of experiences. They may give up interests that once excited them. They may become progressively less joyful and more depressed, ending up with a sense of futility about life. They may even become vindictive, taking pleasure in hurting others becoming a way for them to feel alive.

I have occasionally seen this kind of vindictive behavior when asked to advise family businesses. A typical pattern is where the owner seems to be unwilling to take the steps needed to assure a seamless succession. Given the owner's narcissistic disposition, he (it is usually a he) appears to engage in magical thinking, pretending that death visits everybody else, but not him. In his unconscious, he may imagine himself to be immortal. It is as if he is playing the mythical King Laius, fearful that the next generation will usurp his power. Consequently, he will do everything he can to make life miserable for his successors. Usually, the ending turns into a real Greek tragedy, with a wounded son or daughter, and a ruined enterprise.

The developmental psychologist Erik Erikson formulated the psychosocial theory of human development, explaining that people progress through a series of crises as they grow older. He suggested that once an individual reaches the latest stages of life, they reach the level he termed "ego integrity." Ego integrity is when we come to terms with our one and only life and learn to accept it; in other words, we go through a positive life review, experiencing a sense of coherence and wholeness in reviewing our life. But only when we can find meaning in our life will we reach this integral stage. This will not be the case if we see our life as a series of failed or missed opportunities; if we see our life as unproductive; when we regret our past or feel that we did not accomplish our life goals. If that's the case, we may become subject to depression and hopelessness. In comparison (according to Erikson), people who have reached this integrity stage will not be so troubled by death anxiety. Feelings of despair are less likely to occur.[8]

In the context of death denial, terror management theory has been introduced into the psychological domain. But in spite of its attention-seeking name, I see this theory as yet another way of organizing the various thoughts we have about death anxiety. Basically, it consists of a number of social psychological propositions that draw from existential, psychodynamic, and evolutionary theories to help us understand how our concerns about mortality

[8] Erik H. Erikson (1963), *Childhood and Society*. New York: W. W. Norton.

affect our behavior.[9] And like many others interested in this topic, the exponents of terror management theory view meaning as the fundamental ingredient that buffers (and hence, basically helps us to avoid) the experience of existential anxiety.

Many of these ideas are based on the work of Ernest Becker, a cultural anthropologist who suggested that the human motivation to stay alive, coupled with the awareness that death can occur at any moment, has the power to engender a paralyzing fear of death. He has suggested that "the basic motivation for human behavior is our biological need to control our basic anxiety, to deny the terror of death," once again pointing out that humans spend a great deal of psychological energy on their attempts to manage or deny their subconscious terror.[10] But according to this theory, our cultural worldviews and our self-esteem can serve an important anxiety-buffering function in order to manage (or "tranquilize") our existential fear of death. Furthermore—I previously touched on this earlier—shared symbolic conceptions of reality may also provide a sense of permanence, order and meaning, such as believing in an afterlife or identifying with personal achievements and continuity through family.

Immortality Systems

Given that we're all dying, while lying to ourselves that we're all living forever, we may unconsciously try to convince ourselves that this is actually true; that we will somehow be the exception to the rule; that we will be able to cheat the system and go on living. This is our attempt to turn that ephemeral, terrifying threat of nothingness—into something that may seem to be more manageable, something that can be pinned down. At a conscious level, however, given our apprehension about death, we try to find ways to attain more literal or symbolic immortality. Of course, we can always resort to a faith-based belief in immortality. Generally speaking, religious belief represents the most powerful form of the denial of death. It can be described as the mother of all immortality systems. Symbolically, we can observe how many people embrace a religious dogma to maintain the hope or promise of an afterlife. And these

[9] Greenberg, J., & Arndt, J. (2012). Terror Management Theory. In P. A. M. Van Lange, A. W. Kruglanski, and E. T. Higgins (Eds.), *Handbook of Theories of Social Psychology* (p. 398–415); Solomon, S., Greenberg, J., & Pyszczynski, T. A. (2015). *The Worm at the Core: On the Role of Death in Life.* New York: Random House.

[10] Ernest Becker (1973). *The Denial of Death.* New York: The Free Press.

thoughts may help them to attain a certain peace of mind. At the same time, wars and other forms of strife are examples of how the immortality projects of some people, in particular religion or some kind of ideology, can conflict with those of others.

Of course, many of us deal with the terror of death biologically by living on through our children and grandchildren. We believe that in this way we will pass on our ideas, our cultural artifacts. We can find meaning in devotion to family, friends, and the wider community. Finding community can be an important meaning-maker by creating a sense of immortality. And there is also the symbolic immortality that's fostered through the imagination, by creative work in art, literature, and science. Living on through our achievements can be a very constructive way of dealing with the terror of death. As the poet Ralph Waldo Emerson once said, "Death comes to all, but great achievements build a monument which shall endure until the sun grows cold."

Human civilization can be viewed as the outcome of many of these immortality projects. Wherever we look, we are surrounded by the immortality projects of the generations of people who came before us. For example, we can see the denial of death in action in political, sporting, and business achievements. In the case of the latter, however, the drive to accumulate power and wealth is often motivated by a misguided belief that equates power and wealth with invincibility—with another form of symbolic immortality. In these instances, we can see how people defend themselves against the fear of death by attempting to gain control over others and by achieving financial success.

Another defensive maneuver against death anxiety is to focus on the importance of being part of nature. The assumption is made that when we die, we return to nature, which (before global warming became all-threatening) was supposed to endure forever.[11] Thus, gerotranscendence is associated with a feeling of communion—the experience of an increased feeling of unity with the universe, going through this cycle of generation, degeneration, and regeneration. We have life, we live, and then we give it back.

Another sign of our times is the way people use increasingly sophisticated versions of self-nourishing and toxic habits to relieve emotional pain, in particular death anxiety. Addictive behaviors and substance abuse are alternative magical ways of denying death. But although our conscious fears of death may be temporarily alleviated by these various immortality projects—death anxiety will always be there at an unconscious level.

[11] Manfred F. R. Kets de Vries, (1978). Defective Adaptation to Work: An Approach to Conceptualization, *Bulletin of the Menninger Clinic*, 42 (1), pp. 35–50.

Our fear of death lies at the core of many psychological disturbances, as well as being a basic motivation for living. However, the irony of the human condition is that we like to be free of death anxiety and the fear of annihilation. Paradoxically, being alive awakens this anxiety, limiting the ability of some people to live a full life. The prospect of our death will always tempt us to tranquilize ourselves to lead—at least, superficially—a non-reflective life. Consequently, many people try to deny death by becoming fully absorbed in their social role and striving for whatever their society deems most desirable. And all too often, this turns out to be sex, money, power, status, and fame. Furthermore, death as a stealth motivator may also explain why the people who are most alive are often those who've been diagnosed with a terminal illness and those who have endured a near-death experience. Most probably, they have found ways to come to terms with death. They are able to live with death in the forefront of their lives. And with death acknowledged rather than repressed, these people live their lives more intensely, again indicating that meaning is the flip side of death.

6

In Search of Answers

Gilgamesh, where are you hurrying to?
You will never find that life for which you are looking.
When the gods created man, they allotted to him death.
But life they retained in their own keeping.
As for you, Gilgamesh, fill your belly with good things;
Day and night, night and day, dance and be merry, feast and rejoice.
Let your clothes be fresh, bathe yourself in water.
Cherish the little child that holds your hand.
And make your wife happy in your embrace.
For this too is the lot of man.
—The Epic of Gilgamesh

A man with outward courage dares to die; a man with inner courage dares to live.
—Lao Tzu

In the context of death, philosophers have spent countless hours considering the concept of meaning, including the "meaning of meaning." They have tried to arrive at some kind of coherent understanding of what meaning is, how it is made, and how we can find it. They have also pondered the question whether the meaning of life is internal, inherent in life's many activities, or external—that somewhere in the universe there is a higher entity that we need to answer to.

Around 2000 BCE, Gilgamesh, the hero of the famous epic poem from ancient Mesopotamia was already wondering why he had to die. A similar question was asked by the composers of the *Rig Veda,* a collection of Sanskrit hymns, one of the world's oldest religious texts, composed around

M. F. R. Kets de Vries, *Quo Vadis?*, The Palgrave Kets de Vries Library,
https://doi.org/10.1007/978-3-030-66699-6_6

1700–1100 BCE. In the Old Testament of the Bible (key texts written from the seventh century BCE), Job asks God why he has to suffer and even welcomes death: "Truly man has a term of service on earth; his days are like those of a hireling—like a slave who longs for shadows, like a hireling who waits for his wage. So, I have been allotted months of futility; nights of misery have been apportioned to me."[1] In China, many centuries before Christ, the Taoists questioned the meaning of everything. Around 500 BCE, Buddha wondered how he could overcome suffering. Many of the ancient Greek philosophers focused on reasons for living.

The ancient Greeks believed in the concept of *eudaimonia*, which is best translated as happiness or welfare, and can also be understood as human flourishing or prosperity. In their efforts to understand meaning, the concepts of happiness and meaning became intertwined. Happiness, however, was supposed to be the meaning and purpose of life, the aim and end of human existence. But the concept of *eudaimonia* was expounded upon by Socrates, the Stoics and most extensively Aristotle. While each of their interpretations of *eudaimonia* differed in the details, there was a strong consensus that attaining virtue was necessary to achieve *eudaimonia*. Aristotle, in his book *Nichomachean Ethics*, suggested that the *eudaimon* life was not achieved through pleasure but through "virtuous activity in accordance with reason."[2] He viewed it as a state of serene and permanent happiness, rather than the momentary exaltation of the senses. And even though thousands of years have passed since these ideas were first proposed, the teachings of Socrates, Plato, and Aristotle have continued to shape how we look at well-being and meaning, viewing them as internal processes.

In contrast to the Hellenistic philosophers, the more theologically inclined, such as Augustine of Hippo, Baruch Spinoza, and Paul Tillich, to name just three, believed in an external force—the existence of a God that created the universe. In their search for meaning, religion came to the rescue. According to theists, all of us are in this world for a reason. God created the universe, having a purpose in doing so. But what this purpose is, is only known to God.

People who subscribe to this *Weltanschauung* claim that there is a realm to which life leads us after death. They imagine that all of us will be assessed when our time is up, on the basis of how virtuous or unrighteous we have been during our life on Earth. After our death, depending on God's judgment, rewards or punishments will follow. According to these believers, we are

[1] Holy Bible (1973). New International Version, *Job*, 7:1–3.

[2] Aristotle, *Nichomacean Ethics*, Book I, Chapter 10.

here on Earth to serve or submit to God, and to fulfil the purpose for which God has made us. For theists, it is the existence of God that creates meaning. If there were no God to give ultimate meaning, value, and purpose to our lives, our lives would be absurd. Only God can make us greater than our own individual existence. Living according to God's will is the only way to transcend death.

In contrast to the theologically inclined, some of the philosophers of the Age of Enlightenment took a less mystical and more rational point of view, suggesting that human life has absolutely no meaning. Reason and logic need to replace religion and superstition. According to these thinkers, religion, mysticism and magic all spring from the same fundamental and desperate human need to find meaning in response to the incomprehensibility of having to die. For this reason, Homo sapiens has always struggled to find the meaning of life, trying to find answers in supernatural processes, magic, and other irrational belief systems. Meaning, according to Enlightenment thinkers, should no longer be considered a default position bestowed on us by an all-powerful creator; rather, it is something we discover through logical deduction and reasoning. The conclusion we can draw from this line of reasoning is that it is up to us to create meaning. For example, for the philosopher Friedrich Nietzsche, the Enlightenment eliminated the actuality of a God. He even used the phrase "God is dead." And the philosopher Martin Heidegger, later amplifying Nietzsche's thoughts, wrote: "If God, as the supra-sensory ground and goal, of all reality, is dead; if the supra-sensory world of the Ideas has suffered the loss of its obligatory, and above it, its vitalizing and up-building power, then nothing more remains to which Man can cling, and by which he can orient himself."[3]

Many of these philosophers, influenced by the theories of Charles Darwin, pointed out that the existence of our species should be seen merely as the culmination of evolutionary processes that occurred without a goal or purpose. Faced with the unfathomable vastness of the universe, human beings are just insignificant particles. To suggest that our existence is even part of some divine, external cosmic plan should be viewed as a delusion. In essence, taking this science-based worldview, life on our planet is a meaningless accident in a universe, indifferent to our existence. Human beings better realize that they are alone in the universe's unfeeling immensity out of which they have emerged only by chance.

[3] Martin Heidegger: *Nietzsche's Word, God is Dead.* https://cupdf.com/document/heidegger-nietzsches-word-god-is-dead-holzwege.html p. 163.

With the development of the Big Bang theory—cosmologists' best attempts to reconstruct the 14-billion-year story of the universe—the theists' approach to meaning (despite the rationalization of "intelligent design") became even more questionable. If Earth were destroyed (the route we seem to be on presently), it would be business as usual for the rest of the universe. It would make not the slightest difference. To add insult to injury, Homo sapiens would not be missed. Given these more scientific points of view, existentialist-oriented philosophers and writers (including Friedrich Nietzsche, Søren Kierkegaard, Fyodor Dostoevsky, Franz Kafka, Karl Jaspers, Edmund Husserl, Martin Heidegger, Maurice Merleau-Ponti, Jean-Paul Sartre, Albert Camus and others) went as far as saying that there is something infantile in the presumption that some entity—in the form of a God—has the responsibility of giving meaning to our lives. It is up to us.[4]

What these existentialists emphasized, however, is that we have free will. Each of us has the responsibility to create meaning for our life. As life is not determined by a supernatural god or some other unearthly authority, we are free to choose. *We* need to give our life meaning through our actions, as there's no meaning or purpose imposed on us from outside. We have to discover meaning within ourselves.

According to these philosophers, Homo sapiens' search for meaning should be seen as an internal process. Meaning is unique and subjective to each of us, depending on our particular circumstances and our understanding. *Our meaning of our life is what we decide to make it.* The mythologist Joseph Campbell emphasized this point: "Life has no meaning. Each of us has meaning and we bring it to life. It is a waste to be asking the question when you are the answer." He added: "The meaning of life is whatever you ascribe it to be. Being alive is the meaning."[5]

These very diverse reflections on what meaning is all about are what make our search for meaning so difficult. They also negate the issue of whether there is one overarching meaning to life. It is more realistic to look at meaning as a mosaic concept to which each experience, each facet of our life—family, friends, achievement, recognition, and imagination—contributes a piece. This internal view suggests that it's the contentment we gain from our actions that justifies our life on earth. The rewards for these activities, however, are to be found in the present, in the satisfaction that we experience during our life, rather than in some posthumous spiritual realm.

---

[4] Walter Kaufmann (1975) (ed). *Existentialism from Dostoevsky to Sartre*, Revised and Expanded Edition. New York: New American Library; William Barrett (1990). *Irrational Man: A Study in Existential Philosophy* New York: Anchor.

[5] https://excellencereporter.com/2015/07/21/joseph-campbell-the-meaning-and-the-goal-of-life/.

The proliferation of opinions about what constitutes meaning makes it clear that we humans haven't been very successful in finding answers to the big question of why we are here. Given the mushrooming of ideas, it's no great surprise that the interpretation of our existence varies widely, depending on historical period and dominant school of philosophical thought. Perhaps, to find satisfactory answers to this question, we may have to synchronize our personal ideas of meaning with the prevailing collective ideas—the Zeitgeist—as societies evolve. As long as our personal narrative is in line with the narratives of those around us, it will be easier to convince ourselves whether or not we are living a life of meaning.

The Evolutionary Point of View

In contrast to philosophers, evolutionary biologists offer a more naturalistic view of the meaning of life. According to them, we behave the way we do because we are part of nature. We do what we do because it is part of our genetic wiring. The naturalist Charles Darwin dealt with the question of why we are here as early as 1859 in the context of his theory of evolution. According to Darwin, the basic challenge for all species has always been to prevent its extinction. Therefore, it's actually quite simple to answer questions like why are we here and what is the meaning of life. It has to do with procreation. In other words, meaning comes down to survival and continuance of our species. Essentially, the theory of evolution postulates that organisms adapt to their environment as new, heritable traits that help them survive and reproduce are passed on to their offspring. We behave the way we do because millions of years of evolution have left us programmed to behave in a specific manner. Tor pure evolutionists, the meaning of life is to continue the process of evolution.

This naturalistic explanation of the meaning of life obviously runs counter to the basic religious beliefs of many other people, many of whom eagerly reject evolutionary theory. As a way of thinking about life and death, Darwinian thinking doesn't provide them with the emotional solace they are looking for. The theory of evolution tells us that life existed for billions of years before us; that human life is the product of a lengthy chain of natural events; and that we are not the products of special creation. Darwin made quite clear that there is no grand design instigated by a God, and no such thing as an afterlife. It is not surprising that so many people negate the scientific conclusions that human beings die like any other species, and that there is no scientific proof of a God.

Interestingly enough, the relatively new theory of "intelligent design," implying that there is a purpose to human enterprise becomes a very attractive compromise as it combines wishful thinking about why we are here with a dose of rationality. The theory of intelligent design holds that certain features of the universe and of living things are best explained by an intelligent cause, not as an undirected process like natural selection.[6] However, these pseudoscientific arguments about life's origins and the existence of God are of questionable value.

It is very hard to contest the fact that we are animals with an instinct for survival. At a most basic level, our survival needs come down to food, drink, and rest. And typically, we seek out the opposite sex to procreate. This explains why the answer to questions about the meaning of life has always been disarmingly simple for evolutionists: mating. From this perspective, it isn't a great surprise that having children and family often comes at or near the top spot when people talk about what makes their life worth living—and what provides meaning. As Albert Einstein said: "Our death is not an end if we can live on in our children and the younger generation. For they are us; our bodies are only wilted leaves on the tree of life."

Herd and Attachment-Like Behavior

The notion that humans developed the way we did because it contributed to our ability to reproduce doesn't necessarily mean that we should devote our lives solely to passing on our genes. Evolutionary theory is also founded on the recognition that evolution is headed somewhere, that it has a trajectory. We can see how evolution on Earth has repeatedly gathered small-scale entities into cooperative organizations on a progressively larger and larger scale. Simple cell structures evolved into increasingly complex structures. Collections of these cells formed multicellular organisms, and these organisms organized into cooperative entities. A similar sequence appears to have unfolded in human evolution: from family groups, to bands, to tribes, to agricultural communities and city states, to nations, to transnational structures, and so on.

Therefore, taking a more sociobiological point of view—remembering that social behavior may have been influenced by evolution—we are also herd animals.[7] For survival's sake we have learned how to operate in highly

[6] Michael Behe (1996). *Darwin's Black Box: The Biochemical Challenge to Evolution.* New York: The Free Press; https://www.livescience.com/9355-intelligent-design-ambiguous-assault-evolution.html.

[7] Edward Wilson (1975), *Sociobiology: The New Synthesis.* Cambridge: Harvard University Press.

coordinated groups. And from an evolutionary perspective, we are also designed to pick up social cues, to be able to coordinate and align our behavior with the people around us. This explains why large numbers of people will act in the same way, at the same time. And although herd behavior may refer to practical procedures similar to those found in the animal kingdom, such as looking for food, shelter, and sexual partners, we also find other kinds of herd behavior in humans, expressed through demonstrations, riots, strikes, sporting events, religious gatherings, mob violence, and the way in which social media content goes viral.

This evolutionary herd behavior may also explain why we have such a strong need to bond with others; in other words, it demonstrates the importance of our attachment needs.[8] Once more, it reiterates the fact that Homo sapiens is foremost a social animal. We have a deep need to connect to others, to be part of a group, to sense that we belong, and that we have people who care about us. Thus, taking an evolutionary perspective once again, meaning may not only come down to procreation, it also seems to derive from a strong need to relate to others—to belong.[9] And as social animals, there will be a defined structure for interaction and connectivity between groups of people that goes beyond the basic necessities of survival.

To cut a long story short, do the evolutionary biologists have the answer to the conundrum of meaning? Is life only about satisfying our basic needs? Satisfying our most basic needs may promote temporary satisfaction but does it provide meaning? Does it help us to overcome our death anxiety? I think that there must be more to human life than procreation. I'm drawn to the words of the psychoanalyst Carl Jung: "A human being would certainly not grow to be seventy or eighty years old if this longevity had no meaning for the species. The afternoon of human life must also have a significance of its own and cannot be merely a pitiful appendage to life's morning."[10] Jung might not have realized that this comment points out the importance of attachment-like behavior—of belonging—for the continuity of our species. Furthermore, it adds relationship building—creating a sense of community—to what makes life truly meaningful.

[8] John Bowlby (1988). *A Secure Base: Parent-Child Attachment and Healthy Human Development.* New York: Basic Books.

[9] John Bowlby (1969), *Attachment and Loss, Vol. 1: Attachment.* New York: Basic Books.

[10] Carl Jung (1960), *Collected Works,* Volume 8, The Structure and Dynamics of the Psyche: The Stages of Life, Princeton: Princeton University Press, p. 787.

7

Psychologists to the Rescue

Our dead are never dead to us, until we have forgotten them.
—George Eliot
No one is actually dead until the ripples they cause in the world die away.
—Terry Pratchett

Psychology has always been the science of behavior and mind. With this in mind, meaning, viewed as a psychological concept, has always played an important role in our understanding of human behavior. No wonder that psychologists are preoccupied with questions like: Who am I? Why do I (and people in general) behave the way I (they) do? What motivates my actions? As I suggested before, we will all have individual answers to the question of the meaning of life. But this also implies that if we don't understand what we are all about, we will never be able to find meaning. The search for meaning needs to start with a discovery within. Putting on my psychoanalyst's hat, before defining what you want, you should find out who you are and what makes you tick.

Psychologists also suggest that if we experience meaning in our lives—if we are able to find a set of life goals that give a sense of significance to our existence—pursuing these goals may support our mental and physical health. In comparison, experiencing a lack of meaning has been associated with a number of psychological disorders and even suicidal ideation. No wonder that feelings of meaninglessness motivate people to seek psychotherapy. We search for meaning to find explanations for our suffering, our feelings of guilt, our regrets, our anger, and our fear of death.

Finding meaning very much depends on "who" we are; but finding out who we are requires an inner journey into the self. It implies discovering what

M. F. R. Kets de Vries, *Quo Vadis?*, The Palgrave Kets de Vries Library,
https://doi.org/10.1007/978-3-030-66699-6_7

we stand for and exploring what drives us. It necessitates unearthing our special gifts, desires, and concerns. Thus, when we feel something lacks meaning or seems meaning*less*, it is very often because whatever we're doing doesn't resonate with what's going on deep inside us. For example, we might be engaged in activities that don't fit with who we think we are. Therefore, searching for, discovering, and connecting with our true nature or core essence is imperative to help us find meaning in our lives. We need to engage in a process of self-examination and explore the scripts we are following in our unconscious life.

The founder of psychoanalysis, Sigmund Freud, struggled with the question of free will versus determinism—the extent to which we are able to decide for ourselves to act or to behave in certain ways, or whether our behavior is the result of forces over which we have no control. Freud seemed to support determinism, in that he suggested that our actions and thoughts are controlled from the inside by primitive unconscious instinctual drives and significant childhood events. His propositions became known as psychic determinism. But he also believed that we are capable of making rational decisions and judgments. After all, the goal of psychoanalysis has always been to enable patients to overcome the forces of the unconscious—to help them gain greater control over their life. A completely deterministic point of view would negate that possibility. Freud had to come to terms with the fact that without the belief that people can change, there would be no point in undertaking psychoanalysis or psychotherapy.

Freud also suggested that two major forces rule our psychic life. The first he termed *Eros*, or the life instinct, which includes our sexual instincts, the drive to live, and other basic instinctual impulses. The second, its counterpart, he termed *Thanatos*, the death instinct—the urge toward the destruction or the dissolution of life. According to Freud, we are all in thrall to Thanatos, or the death drive. In other words, the goal of life is death. Both of these fundamental drives, Eros and Thanatos, however, are part of our makeup from the moment we enter the world.[1]

Freud's contemporary, Carl Jung, viewed meaning as central and vital to the fullness of the human experience. According to Jung, as the idea of nothingness is unacceptable to human beings, we have no option but to search for meaning. All of us want to discover the overall patterns that determine our life. We are always looking for understanding and explanations. Homo

[1] Sigmund Freud (1920). Beyond the pleasure principle. In J. Strachey, ed. & trans., *The Standard Edition of the Complete Psychological Works of Sigmund Freud*, Vol. 18. London: Hogarth Press, pp. 3–64; Sigmund Freud (1930). Civilization and its discontent. In J. Strachey, ed. & trans., *The Standard Edition of the Complete Psychological Works of Sigmund Freud*, Vol. 25. London: Hogarth Press, pp. 59–146.

sapiens is compelled to transcend an animalistic existence. Jung even went so far as to suggest that our relentless longing to find a sense of meaning is an archetypal quest: "In the same way the body needs food, and not just any kind of food but only that which suits it, the psyche needs to know the meaning of its existence—not just any meaning, but the meaning of those images and ideas which reflect its nature and which originate in the unconscious."[2] Jung also noted that "a psychoneurosis must be understood, ultimately, as the suffering of a soul which has not discovered its meaning."[3] Furthermore, he suggested that many people suffer from a failure of meaning, characterized by pathological boredom or depression.

Alfred Adler, another psychologist within the analytical tradition, was also preoccupied with humankind's search for meaning. To Adler, the meaning of life is social interest, or as he named it, *Gemeinschaftsgefühl* (community feeling). All of us function in an attempt to achieve something. We want to create something for the good of all. Therefore, the meaning of life cannot be found anywhere except in the creative, useful achievements of the individual. Adler wrote, "We are not determined by our experiences but are self-determined by the meaning we give to them; and when we take particular experiences as the basis for our future life, we are almost certain to be misguided to some degree. Meanings are not determined by situations. We determine ourselves by the meanings we ascribe to situations."[4] To him, transcending pure selfish concerns stands central.

Our attitude toward meaning will change as we progress through life. Where we find ourselves during our lifespan can make a difference in our outlook. Erik Erikson was one of the few psychologists who looked at human development (including meaning making) across the entire course of a person's lifespan.[5] He proposed that we traverse eight distinctive developmental stages as we grow and change throughout life. According to Erikson, at each stage of our psychosocial development, we are faced with a crisis that acts as a turning point in our development. Successfully resolving each crisis will contribute to our overall psychological well-being. At the eighth stage, where integrity stands opposite despair, the key conflict centers on questioning whether or not we have led a meaningful, satisfying life. At this stage we begin to tackle the problem of our mortality. The onset of the eighth stage is often

[2] Carl Jung (1967). *Collected Works*, Volume 13. Princeton: Princeton University Press. P. 476.

[3] Carl Jung (1956), Psychotherapists or the clergy, *Pastoral Psychology*, 7 (3), 27–41.

[4] Alfred Adler (1932/2009). *What Life Could Mean to You: The Psychology of Personal Development.* New York: Oneworld Publications; http://pws.cablespeed.com/~htstein/tp-7b.htm.

[5] Erik Erikson (1950). *Childhood and Society.* New York: Basic Books.

triggered by dramatic life events, such as retirement, the loss of a spouse, the death of friends and acquaintances, physical disability, and other life changes. It is the time when we need to face the fact that we are steadily disintegrating, physically and mentally.

Influenced by psychoanalytic ideas and Zen Buddhist concepts, the philosopher, social psychologist and psychoanalyst Eric Fromm also emphasized the importance of meaning in life. Like many other existential philosophers before him, he suggested that there is no meaning to life except what we give it through our own powers. Living a good life is all about the art of functioning as a whole person. According to Fromm, Homo sapiens' challenge is to find psychological and spiritual happiness by going beyond narcissistic selfishness and egotism. However, in our present-day world, this isn't easy. With the rise of materialism has come a tendency for people to focus on possessing rather than "being." In his book *The Art of Being*, Fromm wrote: "The goal of living [is] to grow optimally according to the conditions of human existence and thus to *become* fully what one potentially *is*; to let reason or experience guide us to the understanding of what norms are conducive to well-being, given the nature of man that reason enables us to understand."[6] Thus, well-being through finding meaning is achievable only to the degree to which we are able to overcome our narcissistic illusions; to the degree to which we are open, responsive, and sensitive; to the extent that we are able to overcome separateness and alienation. Fromm added that the majority of people have not yet acquired the kind of maturity needed to exist as independent human beings. For Fromm, this explains why we need myths and idols to endure the fact that human beings are responsible to themselves; that there is no authority that will give meaning to our life except what we do with it ourselves. It is also the reason why we are too often inclined to surrender our free will to dictators of all kinds, or to lose it by transforming ourselves into a small cog in the machine, well-fed, and well-clothed, yet behaving like an automaton.

However, the psychologist most widely credited as a pioneer in the study of meaning is Victor Frankl.[7] Frankl challenged Freud's propositions by asserting that the search for meaning is the primary intrinsic motivation of humanity, suggesting that humans are more than mechanical beings driven by instinctual drives. Drawing on his horrific personal experiences in Nazi concentration camps during World War II, Frankl developed the more optimistic psychological practice of logotherapy—a form of therapy that is based on the

---

[6] Erich Fromm (1994), *The Art of Being*. London: Bloomsbury Academic.

[7] Victor Frankl (1955), *The Doctor and the Soul*, New York: Knopf; Victor Frankl (1959). *Man's Search for Meaning*. New York: Random House; Victor Frankl (1967). *Psychotherapy and Existentialism*. New York: Simon & Schuster;

premise that human beings are driven to find a sense of meaning and purpose in life. In contrast to Freud's "depth psychology," which emphasizes delving into our past and unconscious desires, Frankl practiced a kind of "height psychology," with a greater focus our future and conscious actions toward achieving a desired future. He suggested that it is up to each of us to actualize what we would like to do—and who we would like to be.

Frankl's experiences as a survivor made him aware that fellow prisoners who had a sense of purpose showed greater resilience to the torture, slave labor, and starvation to which they were subjected. He observed that the greatest difference between those who did and didn't survive the camps was not how much they were forced to work, how little they had to eat, or how exposed they were to the elements. Rather, those who found some meaning or purpose even in those conditions were more likely to survive. In comparison, the inmates who lost meaning were almost certainly doomed. This led Frankl to advocate the idea that people could find meaning even in the worst conditions known to humanity.

Writing of his terrible experiences later in life, he found a partial explanation for this resilience in a quote from Friedrich Nietzsche: "Those who have a 'why' to live, can bear almost any 'how.'" He realized that although he was reduced to a living skeleton, the Nazis could not take one thing away from him: his freedom to choose his attitude. He wrote, "For the meaning of life differs from man to man, from day to day, and from hour to hour. What matters, therefore, is not the meaning of life in general but rather the specific meaning of a person's life at a given moment."[8] He maintained that a strong sense of meaning is essential for optimal human development. It is only through meaning that we make sense of our existence. And in life we find meaning through purposes that will make living worthwhile.

Other major schools of psychology pursue the subject of meaning, notably the humanistic, positive, and existential schools. Humanistic and positive psychologists tend to focus more on human strengths, emphasizing the brighter side of human functioning, whereas existential psychology traditionally addresses the more unsettling aspects of human existence, such as choice, guilt, regret, doubt, suffering, and mortality.

The main assumptions of humanistic psychologists are that humans have free will. By free will, they refer to the choices we make in life, the paths we chose and their consequences. For example, humanistic psychologists such as Abraham Maslow and Carl Rogers suggest that freedom is not only possible but also necessary if we want to be fully functional human beings. Maslow

[8] Victor Frankl (1959). *Man's Search for Meaning*, p. 99

thought meaning would arise from self-actualization or achieving our full potential. Rogers believed that all people had the potential to self-actualize if they achieved their goals, wishes, and desires in life. Both psychologists viewed self-actualization as a unique human need and form of motivation that sets us apart from all other species.

Similarly, the advocates of positive psychology view the search for meaning as a crucial resource for human functioning, striving, and flourishing.[9] This school of thought dwells on topics like character strengths, optimism, life satisfaction, happiness, well-being, emotional intelligence, mindfulness, flow, compassion (as well as self-compassion), gratitude, self-esteem and self-confidence, hope, optimism, wisdom, and positive relationships. Positive psychologists focus on the kinds of behaviors that allow us to build a life of meaning and purpose—to move beyond surviving toward flourishing.

Positive psychology has also a somewhat different orientation from the more traditional schools of psychology. Rather than emphasizing human shortcomings it focuses on human potential. This is why the main emphasis of this field of psychology is on the scientific study of happiness, a flourishing life and well-being, rather than on stress, trauma, and dysfunction. All things considered, positive psychologists tend to focus on what makes life worth living. Critics of this orientation have suggested, however, that the positive psychologists' orientation is too biased toward an over-optimistic view of life, which is, as I have suggested many times over, anything but a rose garden.

Thus, while positive psychology focuses on human strengths and positive emotions and tends to emphasize the "brighter" side of human functioning, we can see how more existentially oriented psychologists such as Victor Frankl, Roland Laing, and Irvin Yalom would emphasize the "darker" or more unsettling aspects of human existence.[10] In that respect, the existential psychological approach has a solid philosophical foundation. It has been influenced, in particular, by the philosophical work of Karl Jaspers and Martin Heidegger and by the work of two psychiatrists, Ludwig Binswanger and Medard Boss, who turned from psychiatry to philosophy in an attempt to better understand the human predicament, its paradoxes and conflicts.

By and large, existential psychology is concerned with understanding people's position in the world and with the clarification of what it means to be alive. And in their search for answers, existential psychologists look for ways of dealing with emotional distress and improve their clients' capacity for

[9] Martin Seligman (2002). *Authentic Happiness: Using the New Positive Psychology to Realize your Potential for Lasting Fulfilment.* New York: The Free Press.

[10] Irvin Yalom (1980). *Existential Psychotherapy.* New York: Basic Books.

self-awareness, given the inevitable tension between freedom and responsibility. Existential psychologists also try to help people find out what they are all about—in the process assisting them in establishing meaningful relationships. They suggest that people have to accept that anxiety is part of the human condition. They help them to cope with the idea of death and non-being. In their quest for answers, they emphasize the search of meaning, purpose and values in life. The existential orientation promotes the idea of free will and self-determination, with the aim of improving their clients' capacity to make conscious choices and help them develop to their maximum potential.

All these psychological orientations tend to highlight one aspect of human existence and neglect others. Yet, despite their different approaches, humanistic, positive and existential psychology—quite independently of each other—view meaning and meaning awareness as central psychological (and philosophical) factors, relevant to both human striving and human coping, as well as to understanding our place in the world. The advocates of these various schools of thought make it clear that life has no meaning unless we design it ourselves. And they view the search for meaning as the most effective way to deal with the stealth motivator that's death.

I recall a client (I'll call her Lisa) who told me about a dream she had had the night before our appointment. She dreamt she was watching a group of people dancing around a maypole at midsummer, singing "*Små grodorna*"—a traditional Swedish song. All of them seemed to be enjoying themselves. Lisa said the dream reminded her of a summer she once spent in Sweden and the good time she had had there. She added that her real-life midsummer night experience, many years ago, had been quite sexually charged. But in the dream itself, she was merely an observer of what was going on—there was no merry making for her—and the scenery around her suddenly changed. She found herself in the middle of an empty, desert-like landscape that reminded her of Death Valley. Finding herself alone, lost in the middle of nowhere, her heart started to race and she started to panic. What could she do? Was there anybody to help her? Could anyone show her the way to go?

When I asked Lisa to associate to the dream, the main feeling she had was intense anxiety about feeling lost. She associated the maypole—a typical phallic symbol—with sexual imagery but also with her regret at not having children. The dancing and singing, in which she took no part, made her think of all her failed relationships. She missed having a sense of belonging. And not having a meaningful relationship made her feel that she was losing out. The desert-like landscape reminded her of the sterility of her work environment. She talked about her concern whether the activities of the company she was working for were meaningful. Finding herself lost in the middle of Death

Valley she saw as "not good news." She interpreted it as a warning sign about her current situation. Altogether, the dream seemed to reinforce the major reason why she had initially come to see me—her concern about her career trajectory. Like the desert landscape, her work seemed increasingly barren. But so was her private life.

Although this dream, like most dreams, offers many avenues for interpretation, one important one seemed to be Lisa's concern about dying on the job, given the apparent purposelessness of her position. It was providing no meaning—at least for her. And as things stood, she felt socially disconnected, while sexually her life was totally barren.

Most importantly, however, Lisa viewed her dream as a warning sign to do something about her situation. She realized that it was high time for her to create meaning in her life. She wasn't going to find it in her present job, for the sake of which she had totally ignored her private life. In that respect, her dream was a kind of tipping point, a sudden moment of insight that made everything click in her life. The dream made her decide to take greater control over her life. She would start looking for a position with more purpose; that she would pay greater attention to relationship building. She ended by telling me that she saw the truth of my often-repeated observation that life is not a rehearsal.

8

Happiness and Meaning

No man is happy until he is dead.
—Aesychlus

Do not seek death. Death will find you. But seek the road which makes death a fulfillment.
—Dag Hammarskjöld

Given the limited time we have on earth to look for meaning, it is inevitable that the concept of happiness comes to the fore. What makes our lives worth living? Is it a life filled with happiness or a life filled with meaning? Or should it be both? Many people think that happiness is a signifier of meaning. And true enough, there appears to be a high degree of overlap between experiencing happiness and finding meaning. Most people who report the one also report the other. Frequently, the times when people report happiness are also the times when they experience meaning. But although a meaningful life and a happy life could go hand-in-hand, that's not always the case. It doesn't necessarily imply a causal relationship between the two. There can be important differences. Moment-to-moment, happiness and meaning are often decoupled. Only think back to our cliff-hanger of reaching for the strawberry.

A reasonable question, however, is whether just being happy is good enough for most of us. It could very well be that many of us want something more than instant gratification, more than just being happy. As an experience, happiness may be too fleeting. Actually, in many instances, just when we think we've found happiness, it evaporates. Wouldn't it be strange to feel happy all

M. F. R. Kets de Vries, *Quo Vadis?*, The Palgrave Kets de Vries Library,
https://doi.org/10.1007/978-3-030-66699-6_8

the time? Isn't happiness actually a kind of aberration? If we were constantly happy, wouldn't the experience of happiness become meaningless?

Perhaps we should ask ourselves instead what makes for happiness and what makes for meaning. In popular thought, health, wealth, and ease in life all seem to be related to happiness, but not necessarily to meaning. For example, we could associate feeling healthy with happiness but not necessarily with meaning. We might feel ill, but that doesn't mean we can't experience meaning. Having no money could cost us happiness but not necessarily meaning. In other words, experiencing life as easy or difficult may affect our happiness, but not necessarily our sense of meaning. Clearly, meaning is not necessarily connected with health, wealth and comfort, although there's no doubt these can contribute to happiness.

Our efforts to distinguish between happiness and meaning have a very long history. I mentioned Aristotle's preoccupation with this particular conundrum in Chap. 6. Aristotle distinguished between *hedonia*, the ancient Greek word for what behavioral scientists now call happiness, and *eudaimonia*—which can be translated as human flourishing or meaningfulness. To Aristotle, the happy life was defined by seeking pleasure and enjoyment, whereas the meaningful life was associated with much more enduring experiences. Or to be more precise, taking a neurological point of view, hedonic happiness or well-being can be conceptualized as experiencing more pleasure than pain. Neurologists seem to equate happiness with transient emotional states or even spikes of activity in the pleasure centers of the brain. In contrast, the experience of eudaimonia refers to the pursuit and attainment of our life's purpose; dealing with the challenges we meet in our journey through life; the feeling that we are part of a community; and the sense that we have personal growth experiences. Thus, meaning becomes a very special kind of "feeling good" based on reaching our full potential; that we are flourishing in whatever we have chosen to do.

Considering these differences, the question becomes, what do we want from life? Is it feeling good—as the hedonists think—or is it doing and being good, as Aristotle and his intellectual descendants, the virtue ethicists, think? Or, would the best of all worlds be to try to attain both?

From my observations, the mere pursuit of happiness isn't enough for many people. This is the legacy of having a brain that enables us to extrapolate the future. In this context, we could categorize happiness as an emotion that's tends to be experienced in the here-and-now, a kind of temporary experience that fades away. In contrast, meaningfulness has a much broader sweep. It has to do with our past, present, and future—and the interrelationships between these temporal states. It makes the experience of meaning much more robust, much less transitory. Happiness can be seen as the means to an end, while meaning is an end in itself. Happiness fades while meaning accumulates. Meaning is not only about transcending the self, but also about transcending the present moment.

Meaning includes the feeling of contributing to something greater than ourselves. According to numerous philosophers and psychologists, it is to be found in the larger context of our life and community. At the same time, however, meaning is also a very personal experience, as it requires finding out what kinds of activities resonate with our beliefs and value systems—the experiences that makes us feel authentic. And as I have suggested before, finding congruence will necessitate a personal journey into the self. It requires understanding what we are all about—discovering our likes, our dislikes, our desires, our loathings, our strengths, and our weaknesses. Given this requirement, reflective thinking will be positively related to meaningfulness, but not necessarily to happiness. The pursuit of instant happiness doesn't require an in-depth inner journey. The pursuit of meaning, however, does. As one of my clients once said to me, "My life isn't about the search for happiness. It's nice to have happy moments, but that's not enough for me. I need to find meaning in whatever I do. It's the only way I feel really alive. I have discovered that it's meaning that has made the challenges I've had to deal with during my life endurable." My interactions with so many clients over the years have shown me that the more we feel our activities are congruent with our values and beliefs, the more we experience meaning.

Nevertheless, by and large, happiness and meaning reinforce each other. For many people, their sense of meaning and their feelings of happiness tend to overlap. For others, there may be a sense of dissonance—they may be low on happiness but high on meaning. Typically, the more meaning we find in life, the happier we feel, and the more we may feel encouraged to pursue even greater meaning.

I suggest that we could consider happiness to be the consolation prize for those whose lives have not yet found meaning. Of course, some might argue that having this consolation prize is good enough. What's so bad about having our immediate needs satisfied? What's so bad about getting what we want and feeling good about it?

Looking around, we can see that for many the joys of sex and material acquisitions seem to be their reason for living. Yet another differentiation between the two is that happiness is getting what we want, while meaningfulness is related to uniquely long-term human activities, such as developing a personal identity, knowing what we are all about, finding purpose, and a sense of self-actualization—consciously integrating our past, present, and future experiences.

Talking from personal experience, I have a farmhouse in the South of France, an area that has been described as a watering hole for the retired. In this beautiful part of the country I have discovered some of the unhappiest people in the world. Granted, they are well provided for. Granted, they have the material wealth to live the good life. Granted, they have nice villas, beautiful cars, and even yachts. They know how to pamper themselves. They have their personal trainer to keep them in shape; they play golf several times a week; they hang around their swimming pools; they can go to parties every night; they occasionally drink too much, take recreational drugs, or engage in sexual adventures. (I'm aware how judgmental I sound here.) Most of their time, however (again being judgmental), is spent in empty, meaningless activities. They can also be quite selfish. From what I can see, they know how to look out for number one—to take from life as much as they can get away with. Again, bringing my own biases into play, in their pursuit of instant gratification, I don't think they reflect very much on what their life is all about. In fact, I have overheard other observers of this human comedy remarking that their behavior is very much like our close cousins, the chimpanzees: they eat drink, groom, and have sex. A philosopher would question whether that's all there is to life and argue that the insertion of a dose of meaning would enrich their existence. But I'm not so sure that's true. The way they behave could be their way of dealing with their inner demons. As many of them are approaching their "best before date," it could be their way of keeping death anxiety at bay. As the saying goes, *"chacun à son gout"* (each to his own taste).

These reflections remind me of Orson Welles' famous movie, *Citizen Kane,* a story about the corrupting influence of wealth and power, and a cautionary tale about the regrets we may experience at the end of our life. Charles Foster Kane tries to control those around him in the way he controls his media empire, whose purpose in turn is to control the way people think. Kane wants love from the world and goes to extremes to get it, yet never seems to have any love of his own to give. Neither power, affluence, material luxury nor sex make Kane happy. His wealth increasingly isolates him from others, and eventually he ends up completely alone at his castle, Xanadu. As his life comes to an end, his final act is to grasp at a memory from a time before wealth and power fell on him, when he was just a poor boy playing in the snow with his sleigh. The story begs the question what Kane could have done differently during his life. Could he have been less selfish? And if so, how would it have changed his life?

Givers and Takers

In the context of giving and taking, it has been said that If you want a meaningful life, don't ask what the world can offer you, but instead what you can offer to the world. Not surprisingly, giving to others has been associated with meaning rather than with happiness. In contrast, taking from others has been related to happiness but not to meaning. It seems that happiness is related to selfish, "me, me, me" behavior, while meaning is associated with selfless, giving behavior. Actually, delving deeper into these kinds of interpersonal relationships, it appears that happier people tend to avoid difficult or taxing entanglements. Because they live more in the moment, they are more self-centered, and less concerned about others. (Another reminder of my experiences in the South of France.) They tend to be takers. In contrast, people looking for meaning are willing to spent time helping others—even though doing so can be stressful. They tend to be givers. And although being socially oriented appears to be associated with both happiness and meaning, happiness seems to be connected to the benefits received from our social exchanges. In contrast, meaningfulness is more related to what we are prepared to give to others. Engaging in challenging or difficult situations by helping others—doing things that transcend ourselves and our own pleasures—will enhance meaningfulness but not happiness.

Famous figures who worked for the public good, like Mother Theresa and Albert Schweitzer, both recipients of the Nobel Peace Prize, were not looking for personal happiness. They were in pursuit of a higher purpose. They were givers. Thus, self-expression is important to meaning making but not to happiness. We can see, how over and over again, in many instances, the unhappy but meaningful life involves difficult undertakings. Often, it is a life characterized by stress, struggles and challenges. Clearly, pursuing our dreams can be a very rocky ride. But while people with a meaningful life may be unhappy in the moment, generally speaking, by being connected to a higher sense of purpose and value, they will live a life of meaning. In other words, an easy life is rarely meaningful, and a meaningful life is rarely easy.

Meaning without Happiness

As I noted, healthy people are happier than sick people, but the lives of many sick people may not lack meaning. Meaningful lives often involve stress and challenges. At the same time, challenges make life richer, and overcoming them makes life meaningful. But people who have meaningful lives may encounter difficult situations that transcend personal interests and can result in great unhappiness.

The "parenthood paradox" sums up the contrast between happiness and meaning: parents usually report that they are very happy to have children. However, it's highly likely parents living with children will score quite low on measures of happiness.[1] Raising kids—especially teenagers—doesn't always bring happiness. The self-sacrifice implicit in raising children may come at the cost of the very things on which happiness most depends. Another example of meaning without happiness are the lives of revolutionaries, who often suffer years of violence and discord for a larger purpose that might ultimately bring great satisfaction and meaning to their lives and the lives of others. But at what price?

The Dark Side of Meaning

As a caveat to the happiness-meaning equation, I should add that although the pursuit of happiness may not bring meaning, its pursuit shouldn't be ignored. There is a very human quality to the pursuit of happiness. As Voltaire wrote in *Candide*, "*Il faut cultiver notre jardin*" ("we must cultivate our garden"). We should be careful not to take our pursuit of meaning to extremes. I have seen some of my clients become obsessed with doing good. I have pointed out to them, many times over, that in pursuing meaning, they should be careful to manage their ambitions and avoid becoming martyrs to a cause. There is something to be said for taking care of your own immediate needs before trying to take care of everybody else's. It's not for nothing that we're told while being in a plane emergency to set up our own oxygen mask before trying to set up someone else's. Ignoring our own needs is not going to be helpful in the long run. It may just wear us out.

In our pursuit of meaning, we shouldn't ignore the pleasure we can find in the little things of life, like paddling in the sea, smelling the flowers in the garden, watching birds soar in the sky, having a conversation with good

[1] Roy F. Baumeister (1992), *Meanings of Life*. London: Guilford Press.

friends, getting lost in a book, going for a walk in nature, or playing with our children. Feeling good doing these little things can make us feel much better in our skin—and eventually help us to pursue meaning with more energy. Taking everything into account, we should never forget to appreciate the immediacy of being alive, the absolutely amazing fact that we are here right now, breathing, thinking, and doing.

Some people who pursue meaning obsessively should ask themselves whether whatever they are doing could be done on a more human scale. I have dealt with people who try to work on too large a canvas. They would be much better off trying to remain human rather than become superhuman. We don't always need to reach for the sky. What's more, some of them aren't necessarily creating a better world: they may simply have a need to force their *Weltanschauung* on others—not always for the better. Often, in their ideological zeal, they deny others the right to pursue their own sense of meaning.

Because, like many areas of human experience, the pursuit of meaning can have a dark side. Just think about the millions of people whose lives have been sacrificed in the name of meaning. Totalitarian ideologies, for example, create meaning while crushing the desires of individuals and taking away their opportunities for happiness. When we look at the history of humankind, many meaning makers, convinced of the righteousness of their cause, have deemed that the loss of individual well-being is irrelevant. Instead, what seemed to be of overriding importance was to bring what they saw as valuable gains to society at large. Rigorous adherence to some of these ideologies has contributed to the proliferation of immense misery and human suffering. Therefore, it is often wiser to be modest in our aspirations, rather than erase our humanity.

In most instances, as I hope I have shown, meaning and happiness can go hand-in-hand. Having a meaningful life can contribute to happiness; being happy can also contribute to finding life meaningful. Generally speaking, however, if we aspire to being able to look back at a well-lived, happy life—a life of integrity—it makes more sense to pursue the things we find meaningful—the kinds of activities that provide us with not only a sense of mastery but also worthwhile purpose; to look for deep relationships that make us feel good; and to engage in altruistic activities that go beyond narrow self-interest. Over the course of our life, looking for instant pleasures will not be enough. Happiness without meaning leads a relatively shallow, self-absorbed or selfish life, where needs and desires are too easily satisfied, and difficult but life-rewarding experiences are avoided. Our challenge is to find our "sweet spot" of well-being: that magical combination of happiness and meaning that sets a virtuous cycle in motion, and ultimately makes for a life well lived.

9

Meaning, Health, and Well-Being

Happiness is someone to love, something to do and something to hope for.
—Chinese Proverb

Well-being cannot exist just in your own head. Well-being is a combination of feeling good as well as actually having meaning, good relationships and accomplishment.
—Martin Seligman

Finding meaning isn't a luxury. Leading a life of meaning will make a great difference to our quality of life. There are few things more important for our mental health (see Chap. 7). Finding meaning plays a crucial role in healthy development and the way we cope with life's challenges. In other words, meaning in life is strongly correlated to psychological well-being and even longevity. When we experience meaning in life, we tend to have better health and well-being, whatever our age might be. Also, living a purpose-driven, meaningful life makes us more effective in handling difficult situations. Depressive reactions will be less of a problem. We will be more likely to engage in constructive behaviors, and be physically more active. Predictably, adopting a "sportier" lifestyle can reduce the incidence of chronic disease and obesity.[1]

[1] https://www.ncbi.nlm.nih.gov/pmc/articles/PMC4224996/ purposeful individuals lived longer than their counterparts; https://doi.org/10.1037/a0017152 Purpose in Life as a System that Creates and Sustains Health and Well-Being: An Integrative, Testable Theory; https://www.apa.org/news/press/releases/2009/08/positive-educate.

M. F. R. Kets de Vries, *Quo Vadis?*, The Palgrave Kets de Vries Library,
https://doi.org/10.1007/978-3-030-66699-6_9

Quality of Relationships

Interestingly, people who live a life of meaning also have a lower rate of divorce and are less likely to be living alone. On the whole, they are more astute in their social interactions and create more meaningful relationships with family and friends. Their social skills make them more likely to participate in social and cultural activities. This suggests that people in pursuit of meaning are better at relating meaningfully to other human beings. There is an association with a sense of belonging: if our presence and/or absence means something to other people, it will have a positive impact on our mental and physical health.

These findings are confirmed by the "Lives in Progress Study" that originated during America's Great Depression, spanned more than 80 years, and remains the longest study ever carried out on happiness and life satisfaction. According to this study, the good life very much depends on the quality of our relationships.[2] Time spent with others seems to protect us from the stress and vicissitudes of life. When the study started in 1938, a number of researchers at Harvard University began tracking the health of 268 students (all men—Harvard did not admit women at the time). They hoped that a longitudinal study would reveal clues about how to lead a healthy and happy life. After following the surviving Harvard men for more than 80 years, a major finding was that while taking care of our body is undoubtedly important, tending to our relationships appears to be equally important in terms of self-care. The people who fared best during their life were those who leaned into relationships with their family, friends, and community.

This seminal study showed clearly that there appears to be a strong correlation between men's flourishing lives and their relationships with family, friends, and community. However, what the study also showed is that loneliness kills. It seems the difference between having a good life or a miserable life is the quality of our relationships. Intimate relationships are essential to make us feel good in our skin. Close ties with others protect us from life's discontents, help to delay mental and physical decline, and are a better predictor of a long and happy life than social class, IQ, or even genes. Therefore, from a health perspective, people who experience compassion, love, and social support are greatly advantaged.

The "Lives in Progress" study also found that the good life is not about money, fame, power or status; that it is unwise to measure our life in terms of

---

[2] Robert W. White (1972). *Lives in Progress: A Study of the Natural Growth of Personality.* New York: Holt & Co; https://www.health.harvard.edu/blog/the-secret-to-happiness-heres-some-advice-from-the-longest-running-study-on-happiness-2017100512543.

what we own; and that it is a bad idea to be preoccupied by material possessions. In fact, if the acquisition of material goods is our main goal in life, it contributes to the creation of a psychological void that never can be filled. Basically, if we want to live a good life, we better pay attention to our partner, our children, other family members, and our friends. It is relationships with people for whom we have love and affection, and who, in their turn, give us theirs that make life worth living. To quote Victor Frankl, "Man is originally characterized by his 'search for meaning' rather than his 'search for himself.' The more he forgets himself—giving himself to a cause or another person—the more human he is. And the more he is immersed and absorbed in something or someone other than himself the more he really becomes himself."[3] I have observed repeatedly in my work with executives that the way we obtain meaning in our lives is to devote ourselves to appreciating others, and to care about our community. Passing on something of ourselves to others is what makes life truly meaningful. As Tolstoy wrote, "The sole meaning of life is to serve humanity." In a similar vein, Albert Einstein noted: "Only a life lived for others is a life worthwhile."

Altruism and its Evolutionary Origins

Altruistic activities seem to play a significant role in living a long and meaningful life. Altruism is typically defined as the disinterested and selfless concern for the well-being of others. In the words of the Dalai Lama, "Our prime purpose in this life is to help others." Altruism is the practice of engaging in voluntary behavior, rather than doing things with the expectation of a reward. This definition of altruism as compassionate concern for others is closely related to what Erik Erikson described as generativity, that is, a person's concern for the welfare of future generations and for the world at large.[4]

When we think of altruism, we tend to think of those extraordinary men and women who dedicated their lives to improving the conditions of others: Mother Theresa (who ministered to lepers, the homeless and the poorest of the poor in the slums of Calcutta); Sir Nicholas Winton (who organized the *Kindertransport* that helped Jewish children escape from Czechoslovakia during World War II); and, more recently, Denis Mukwege, known as "Doctor Miracle" for his ability to repair through reconstructive surgery the horrific damage inflicted on women who were raped in the Democratic Republic of

---

[3] https://excellencereporter.com/2019/06/21/viktor-frankl-on-the-wisdom-and-the-meaning-of-life/.

[4] Erik H. Erikson (1963), *Childhood and Society.* New York: W. W. Norton.

the Congo. But these are exceptions. Most altruistic behavior takes place on a much more modest scale far away from the media spotlight. For example, many people give a considerable amount of their time to volunteering. Being actively involved in purposeful activities within the community—either helping specific individuals and/or collaborating with others in some joint activity—helps to integrate us into larger society by attaching us to someone or some cause greater than ourselves. This can be an important way of transcending the self. What we do for ourselves alone dies with us; but what we do for others and the world remains and will be remembered.

I will go so far as to suggest that altruism is part of our evolutionary heritage. It is clear that human beings are inclined toward helpful prosocial and altruistic behavior. We could argue—studying how Homo sapiens has evolved—that altruistic behavior within a group makes for a competitive advantage over other groups. There seems to be a powerfully adaptive connection between widely diffuse altruism within groups and group survival. Over and over again, we can see how altruistic behavior positively affects the longevity of group members. According to anthropologists who have studied more egalitarian societies (such as the Inuit or the San Bushmen) institutionalized or "ecological altruism"—helping others—is a social norm. It becomes a generational imperative.

High levels of volunteerism seem to be significantly associated with lower mortality rates.[5] Various medical studies have shown that those who provide more assistance to others are significantly more likely to report that they are in better physical shape. Of course, one factor in the relationship between altruism and health might be that altruistic individuals tend to be more energetic and sociable people who like to be involved in all kinds of social activities, regardless of whether those activities show compassionate concern for others. At times, it may be difficult to distinguish whether we are dealing with genuine altruistic behavior itself or a more general pattern of social engagement. It should be added that good health in itself could influence who becomes altruistic and who will not.

This is a significant caveat; however, it can't be denied that when we help others, we tend to feel better about ourselves, which has positive mental and physiological implications. Essentially, as mentioned before, "giving behavior" seems to offer the giver tangible, long-term mental and physical health benefits. Not only do altruistic activities make for more meaningful social integration, they may also distract us from our personal problems. In

[5] Morris A. Okun, Ellen W. Yeung, E. W., & Stephanie Brown (2013). Volunteering by older adults and risk of mortality: A meta-analysis. *Psychology and Aging, 28*(2), pp. 564–577.

addition, the greater sense of self-efficacy and competence people experience while engaging in such behavior can also have a stress buffering effect.

In this context, I turn again to Carl Jung's question—why do we live so long?—that I referred to in Chap. 6. Why, after we have fulfilled our evolutionary objective—of having and raising children—are we still alive? Jung posed the question because Homo sapiens, in contrast to other species, lives and works well past its reproductive years. Is the reason for our longevity that we still have an evolutionary role to play? Is there still a role for the original caregivers? Could there be such a thing as "social" generativity, disguised as altruism, as older adults are oriented toward helping the younger generation, in particular their grandchildren? From a more socio-biological point of view, our longevity might illustrate natural selection at work, in that these seemingly altruistic activities might improve survival rates for the younger generation. The selective advantage that young people may experience due to grandparenting or other generativity-induced activities, could be one of the explanations why humans outlive our reproductive purpose.

To summarize, positive emotions, helping behavior, or both, are associated with well-being, health, and longevity.[6] Altruistic activities appear to slow down the aging process. These positive emotions (kindness, compassion, philanthropy) may neutralize emotionally and physically harmful negative emotions (such as rage, hatred, and fear). In other words, it is good to be good. Ironically, being selfless can be quite selfish—giving seems to have more positive mental health implications for the giver than for the recipient. Caregiving activities—whether for other people or for the environment—make more altruistically inclined people feel needed. And the feeling that they're making a difference appears to contribute to their mental health. Thus, a generous life makes also for a happier and healthier one.

However, there are questions about the relevance of altruism as a route to meaning that have to be taken into consideration in our contemporary society. There is a real danger that in our social media obsessed world, people have become too isolated to engage in altruistic activities. Also, not all altruistic behavior is necessarily healthy. There are definite adverse health consequences associated with over-giving. As I mentioned in the previous chapter, there are always going to be people who put too much stress on themselves because they are compelled to give beyond what they are able to handle physically and

[6] Stephen G. Post (2005). Altruism, Happiness, and Health: It's Good to Be Good, *International Journal of Behavioral Medicine*, 12, (2), pp. 66–77; Caroline Schwartz, Janis Bell Meisenhelder, Yunsheng Ma, and; George Reed (203). Altruistic Social Interest Behaviors Are Associated with Better Mental Health, *Psychosomatic Medicine*, 65 (5), pp. 778–785.

emotionally. Emotionally overwhelmed, they become exhausted, which has a debilitating effect on their physical and mental health.

Notwithstanding these caveats, there are significant health benefits to altruistic behavior. It is worth repeating that often the greatest purpose in life, the greatest achievement we could ever have, and the greatest satisfaction, can only be found in the service of others. For example, it is heartening to see the meaning-making actions of Millennials and Generation Z, typically inspired by young activists like Greta Thunberg, who are addressing climate change and getting behind initiatives like Black Lives Matter to protect the physical and social environment of our planet.

Gratitude

Gratitude goes hand-in-hand with altruism, and is another activity that's very important for our well-being. While generous acts provide meaning, acknowledging the kindness we receive from others adds to the meaning-making process. Like altruism, gratitude also appears to be good for our mental health.[7] Saying "Thank you" and showing appreciation can do a lot of good on a personal level.

Gratitude is the thankful appreciation for what we receive from others, whether it's tangible or intangible. It is a way of appreciating what we have, instead of focusing on our dissatisfaction with what we don't have. Expressing gratitude disconnects us from toxic emotions, like anger, envy and spite, helps us to deal with life's adversities, and increases our general sense of well-being. In the general run of things, people who count their blessings tend to be happier and less depressed. If we make a real effort, there will always be something for which we can be thankful. It is worth practicing gratitude every day, even to the extent of keeping track of the number of people you say "Thank you" to on a daily basis.

Gratitude is a conscious choice, in that we make the decision to express gratitude; it is not something imposed by others. But when all is said and done, feeling gratitude comes down to a shift in perspective. We can focus on the negative things in life and complain, or we can decide to choose for gratitude and be happy. Every day, in every circumstance, this choice is open to us. By expressing gratitude, we acknowledge the goodness in our lives, helping us connect to something larger than ourselves. And living this way will make for a more meaningful life.

---

[7] https://www.health.harvard.edu/healthbeat/giving-thanks-can-make-you-happier.

A Sense of Competence

Competence is closely related to purpose, so it also plays an important role in the meaning-making process. Feeling competent makes us feel good, mentally and physically. Although tying our self-worth solely to the outcome of what we are trying to accomplish can make for an unstable sense of self-worth, generally speaking, we still prefer the positives of our activities to outnumber the negatives. We want to have the feeling that we are moving forward, progressing, honing our skills—to feel competent in whatever we are doing. Thus, for many people, the meaning of life is related to progressing, to achieving, to becoming better at what they do. Competence is also about taking pride in what we can accomplish. In short, it makes us feel better.

But again, it is of utmost importance that we experience the activities in which we are involved as meaningful. As the saying goes, people work for money but die for a cause. In this respect, real work can provide a lot of meaning. Life would be very empty without it. Although we are often taught to think of ourselves as inherently selfish, the longing to act meaningfully seems just as stubborn a part of our make-up. Engaging in meaningful work has a positive effect on our mood.

If possible, we should try to do the kind of work that helps us to help others. Work is at its best when people feel at their best, making it important that they bring their whole selves to work. I am not referring just to people in the helping professions (some of these people can also be quite selfish). There are many ways in which we can contribute to the common good in the workplace. Unfortunately, I have encountered many people who never truly live because they don't do what they truly love, either by design or involuntarily. Often, it doesn't dawn on them that they have a choice. To sum up, the meaning of life is to matter, to make a difference. When the time comes for us to go, we should leave the world a better place than it was when we were born.

10

The Art of Meaning-Making

I have always believed, and I still believe, that whatever good or bad fortune may come our way we can always give it meaning and transform it into something of value.
—Hermann Hesse

The least of things with a meaning is worth more in life than the greatest of things without it.
—Carl Jung

Mark Twain once said, "The two most important days in our life are the day we're born and the day we find out why." Of course, this begs the question of what we are going to do with ourselves during the interim. Throughout this book, I have suggested that what makes a human life meaningful is not merely living a life but also reflecting on living a life. In particular, it is hard to endure our own littleness unless it can be translated into some form of meaningfulness. If life appears meaningless, we easily fall into despair. We may get depressed by all the dysfunctional repercussions. As I have said repeatedly, a life of meaning is beneficial to our mental and physical health.

Earlier in this book I wrote that the question "Why are we here?" will haunt most of us throughout our lives. It compels us to place our life in a larger context—to develop narratives that contain meaning. All of us like to tell a congruous story of what our life is all about. In doing so, however, we should remember not to measure our contribution to the world in terms of status, power, or wealth. It is more sensible to look at our the contribution we make to humanity and the natural world. Dostoyevsky makes this point in his

M. F. R. Kets de Vries, *Quo Vadis?*, The Palgrave Kets de Vries Library,
https://doi.org/10.1007/978-3-030-66699-6_10

novel *The Brothers Karamazov*: "For the secret of human existence lies not only in living, but in knowing what to live for. Without a firm conviction of the purpose of living, man will not consent to live and will destroy himself rather than remain on earth, though he be surrounded by bread."[1]

For many, the combination of a successful career, a loving family, and a strong social network seems to be the prescription for a meaningful life. Others may argue that the purpose of life is to leave a larger legacy—to make an effort to engage in activities that will transcend narrow personal interests. They note that leaving such a legacy is the way to feel valued and to be remembered after we're gone. This doesn't imply achieving something on a grandiose scale, such as building a business empire or winning a Nobel Prize—it could simply mean leaving the world a slightly better place, having made a small contribution to humanity.

Remember Ted, whose case opened this book? Like him, most of us are driven by a need to fill our life with some kind of meaning. To some of us, it's quite clear what this meaning is going to be. For most of us, however, the issue will be much cloudier. Not knowing, however, can lead to a sense of emptiness, of feeling trapped in a void. Often, as I suggested before, when trying to cope with this void, some are tempted to fall into the action trap. They try to fill the gap with dread or pleasure, booze or drugs, religion or vice, action or indolence, love or hatred. Alternatively, they may take a very different, more positive approach, trying to deal with the void by increasing their self-awareness and ascertaining their role in the world.

Many people will choose for the first alternative, however. It is the road more travelled. We can all see how many people sleepwalk through a meaningless life, in spite of busily doing things they imagine are important. In reality, they behave like rats on a treadmill. The French have a nice expression for this condition: "*Métro, boulot, dodo*." This phrase—literally meaning "commute, work, sleep"—is a great way to describe the daily grind to which many of us subject ourselves. Too many people just get up on Monday and do the same thing they've done every single Monday—go to work and function on automatic pilot—without finding any meaning in their life. They're born; they're receive some education; they get a job; they find a mate; they raise kids; they make money; and eventually they die. But they die without having any idea why they were doing what they were doing. In reality, they were not going anywhere. In other words, they have been so busy perfecting the means of travel that they have forgotten where they wanted to go—they don't even ask themselves whether they're enjoying the journey. While they were busily

[1] https://www.goodreads.com/quotes/889146-for-the-secret-of-man-s-being-is-not-only-to.

following the "*métro, boulot, dodo*" cycle, they forgot the main purpose of life: to know themselves better and find out what is the most meaningful to them.

Authenticity

Life has very little purpose for too many people. Like Ivan Ilych, whom I wrote about in Chap. 3, they may come to realize what they have done to themselves only when they're dying. One of the greatest fears of us all is not the inevitability of death but the distinct possibility of realizing we have lived a worthless life. And as we saw with Ted, not knowing the ultimate purpose of why he was on this earth caused him a tremendous amount of misery. When we have no purpose to live for, we are neither the master of our fate nor the captain of our soul. We will not be in control of whatever we're doing. Behaving like passengers on the bus, rather than the bus driver, creates the real possibility that we will be used by other people who know where they want to go, who know what they want out of life, and who are determined to get what they want. But without meaning, we're like lost souls, aimlessly roaming the earth.

But in spite of all the busyness we may create, the question of our life's meaning will inevitably emerge, either unbidden or through conscious intent. In dealing with life's vicissitudes, we can choose either to be passive or to be proactive. We better realize in time that it is important to live authentically. To be true to who we really are will be fundamental to feeling fulfilled and living a life of integrity.

Authenticity implies that our actions are congruent with our beliefs and desires, despite external pressures. It means living in a completely integrated way—being in sync with our own values, beliefs, and principles. It means that we act in ways that show how we truly feel. It entails the courage to be vulnerable, to be willing to show our true self. In whatever we do, the impetus for our actions should come from within rather than being imposed externally. Authenticity also means shedding our biases and seeing ourselves for who we are, in all our contradictory and complex splendor. The golden rule of authenticity is to treat others as we want to be treated. It means feeling comfortable that we are not perfect in the eyes of others, and embracing our weaknesses and quirks. If we behave according to these principles, we will feel much better in our skin.

Another important aspect of living an authentic life is a willingness to address the "why," regardless of whether we believe in the existence of the soul, practice a religion, or are agnostic. And whatever our *Weltanschauung* turns out to be, we need to have the courage to undertake this inner journey. Otherwise, if we just let it be, our lives will more likely than not remain superficial and empty, in spite of our material goods and gains.

The Examined Life

Pursuing ends and goals—fitness, financial success, academic accomplishments—is all well and good, but it doesn't necessarily make for meaningfulness. That isn't because we have the wrong sorts of goals, but rather because we have failed to take up the right sort of reflective perspective on our life. And as I suggested before, a way of safeguarding our mental health is to know what we are all about and what's really important to us. This implies the willingness to embark on an inner journey to discover our strengths, weaknesses, values, beliefs, desires, and the major scripts in our inner theater. It also means having the readiness to accept that beneath the social mask we wear every day, we might have a hidden shadow side: an impulsive, wounded, sad, or isolated part of who we are, an aspect of ourselves that we generally try to ignore. But we should keep in mind that this shadow side can also be a source of emotional richness and vitality. Acknowledging that part of ourselves can be a pathway to healing and to living a more authentic life.

However, many people move through life making little effort or no effort at all to understand what they are all about. Of course, they know about some of the things they like and some things they dislike, but they know very little about what creates meaning for them. They risk dying in ignorance, without ever knowing what's really important, if they never bother to really examine their lives. Preferring not to see creates a life with very little meaning. Unfortunately, in my work as a psychoanalyst, psychotherapist and executive coach, I have met many people who behave this way, who are unwilling to take this route less travelled. Often, their motivation to try to make changes emerges only during times of transition or crisis—for example, a career setback, an educational opportunity, a divorce, a personal loss, or even relocation.

But while we make the journey within ourselves, we may be faced with many unanswered questions. Our challenge is to have the courage to look for answers to these questions. Difficult as this might be, without this kind of soul searching, we won't be going anywhere. We have to take a step back from everyday life and take time out to think about our life in a very different manner. But what we find may not be to our liking. We may discover that our present life has little or no meaning. That's not something anyone likes to hear; most of us want to believe that we are in this world for a reason. But we should not be looking for the meaning of life, which is merely an abstraction; we should be looking for meaning *within* our lives. It is our responsibility to give meaning to our life, not just to be an indifferent bystander.

It must be said that not many people are prepared to undertake this journey to the interior. And even when they try, they may get stuck, as the exploration can trigger a host of resistances. Many prefer not to see what they see. No wonder that much of humanity lives life in complete oblivion, preoccupied by daily activities, while meaning falls by the wayside. Many people don't know how and why they are here, and what they are supposed to do. And many don't even care. As Oscar Wilde put it, "To live is the rarest thing in the world. Most people exist, that is all." But what can we do to live, not just exist? What does it mean to live a full, meaningful, and authentic life?

As I have said before, unlike animals, we possess a reflective capability; we have our human consciousness. With the advanced development of our brains, we have the cognitive and emotive capacity to unravel complex problems. Due to the development of our frontal lobes—that part of the brain that controls important cognitive skills—we have the ability to contemplate the meaning of life. We can extrapolate our developmental trajectory and by doing so realize that our stay on earth is only temporary. Accepting this fact forces us to make choices, and ideally those choices will be congruent with the scripts in our inner theater. The better we know who we are and what we want, the better our choices will be—and acting on these, the more complete we're likely to feel and the more likely we are to live a life of meaning.

Meaning should not be looked at as a luxury problem pursued by a select few. It isn't just a challenge for budding philosophers, it's a challenge for us all. A life of meaning will give us the opportunity to live better, happier, and healthier lives. But taking this road less travelled also implies that we have to be prepared to deal with highs and lows, losses and triumphs, joy and pain, light and shadows, triumphs and tragedies, accomplishments and adversities. A life worth living has to comprise an integrative view of the human condition—the negatives and the positives.

When we realize the transience of our existence, we might be motivated to create something of value that we can give to this world, to matter in some way, to make a little bit of a difference. Just focusing on our most basic needs (like animals), is not going to be good enough. The human animal can do so much more. It is up to us to make a difference in this world, small though the difference may be. Each of us can make an effort at transcendence, and go beyond our own narrow personal concerns. However, this implies that we must be prepared to deal with questions like, who am I? What am I doing here? What is my life's purpose? What's the meaning of it all? Where do I belong? What do I need to do to feel fulfilled? We are here on earth to unearth who on earth we are.

Discovering Meaning

Fortunately, given our confusion about what meaning is all about, psychologists have come to the rescue. In many different ways, and through various psychotherapeutic interventions, psychologists have tried to help us get in touch with lasting values, beliefs, needs and goals, and have tried to build a sense of meaning and purpose around these important parts of our life. Some use specific psychological techniques, such as talking therapy, behavioral interventions, mindfulness meditation, dreamwork, and other powerful interventions, to understand better what meaning means to us.

Probably the best-known psychological method is Victor Frankl's logotherapy.[2] Frankl has indicated repeatedly that human beings create meaning by taking a courageous stance toward life's difficulties even in dire or life-threatening circumstances. As a species, we have the ability to connect with life through art, humor, nature, love, and relationships. Furthermore, we can engage with life through work, hobbies, or other activities. Also, as meaning exists in an historical context, we are able to explore meaning through our understanding of our past and present, and to use this knowledge to think about the future and build a legacy. Logotherapy posits that meaning is based on enduring values that emanate from these various sources.

Frankl used techniques such as "dereflection" (helping clients focus less on themselves and more on higher-level goals, such as helping others) and Socratic dialogue (asking open-ended questions to help clients uncover meaning-related aspirations). He believed that meaning cannot be pursued as a goal in itself. It must ensue as a side-effect of pursuing other goals. Thus, if we want to find meaning, we need to embrace activities that connect us with something greater than ourselves. For example, if one of my clients were concerned about global warming, I would try to help him or her to find concrete ways to contribute to environmental projects. If my client were interested in education, together we would figure out ways to make a meaningful contribution to the field.

---

[2] Victor Frankl (1985). *Man's Search for Meaning*. New York, NY: Washington Square Press/Pocket Books; Victor Frankl (1969). *The Will to Meaning*. New York: Penguin Books.

The psychologist Paul Wong built on Frankl's work. More specifically, he developed "meaning therapy," which he described as an integrative, positive existential approach to counseling and psychotherapy, incorporating elements of cognitive-behavioral therapy, positive psychology and research findings on meaning. He presented his intervention as a comprehensive way to address all aspects of meaning in an individual's life. Using his PURE model (Purpose, Understanding, Responsible action and Enjoyment/Evaluation), Wong tried to help people balance positive and negative elements of life by encouraging them to pursue goals or activities that would be greater than themselves. This intervention technique appeals to people's sense of responsibility to take charge of their life—to pursue their freedom to decide what really matters and what they think will be a satisfying future.[3]

"Meaning-centered" psychotherapy—blending psychology and spirituality—is another form of therapy derived from Frankl's work.[4] It was originally designed to help patients with advanced cancer sustain or enhance a sense of meaning, peace, and purpose, even as they approach the end of their life. Specifically, this intervention technique deals with patients' fear of death by helping them explore what they would consider to be a good or meaningful death. This form of therapy also encourages patients to embrace more positive attitudes about their life, their illness, and their coming death. It also helps them address how they can fulfill their responsibilities courageously, to help them connect with what makes them feel most alive. Most importantly, participants attracted to this form of psychotherapy are encouraged to create "personal legacy projects" to address what is most meaningful to them, such as mending a broken relationship, engaging in some kind of volunteer work or visiting a place they have always wanted to see.[5] Finding their life's purpose, using this therapeutic approach, will clarify where they should put their energy and what are they capable of doing.

Another approach to the search for meaning is existential psychotherapy, which builds on the work of Sigmund Freud, Otto Rank, and Rollo May. For example, Irvin Yalom, one of its foremost representatives, points out that life is inherently random and meaningless. That being the case, humans have the responsibility to create their own sense of meaning.[6] Fortunately, we have the

[3] Paul T. P. Wong, (2008). Meaning-management theory and death acceptance. In A. Tomer, G. T. Eliason, & P. T. P. Wong (Eds.), *Existential and spiritual issues in death attitudes* (pp. 65-87). New York, NY: Erlbaum; Rollo May (1969), *Existential Psychology*, New York: Random House.

[4] William S. Breitbart and Shannon R. Poppito (2014). *Individual Meaning-Centered Psychotherapy for Patients with Advanced Cancer: A Treatment Manual.* New York: Oxford University Press.

[5] William Breitbart (2014). *Psychosocial Palliative Care.* New York: Oxford University Press.

[6] Irvin Yalom (1980). *Existential Psychotherapy.* New York: Basic Books.

free will to think, believe, and rationalize what is true in our mind, a process that can empower us to take action through our free will. In his therapeutic interventions, Yalom emphasizes the human condition as a whole, using a positive approach that applauds human capacities and aspirations while simultaneously acknowledging our limitations. He suggests that the way to create meaning is to engage more fully in life—to take on activities and people we're drawn to and that nurture us. In that respect, existential psychotherapists help their clients to break down barriers to engagement with life by asking them what is preventing them from doing what they really want to do—and what the journey to get there is going to entail.

The psychologist Steven Hayes, taking a behavioral perspective toward helping people find meaning, has introduced what he calls "Acceptance and Commitment Therapy (ACT)."[7] Like meaning and existential therapies, ACT seeks to help clients live full lives and face their existential issues. ACT clients are encouraged to increase their psychological flexibility, in other words, the ability to enter the present moment more fully. In this form of psychotherapy, people are helped to identify their values, choose behaviors that harmonize with those values, and use mindfulness, awareness, and acceptance strategies to deal with the vicissitudes of life. Furthermore, they are strongly encouraged to embrace a passionate and ongoing interest in living these values.

Enjoying the Journey

Given the availability of these various psychological interventions, exploring the meaning of life is not just a cliché that can never be attained. We have many options from which to explore the themes that are important to us. In this search, a critical aspect of the meaning-making process will be to find purpose. And discovering our purpose is not just an afterthought. Our life will never contain meaning if we don't have a goal or purpose.

As I wrote in Chap. 1, having a purpose means doing something valuable, engaging in something significant. Purpose can guide our life decisions, influence our behavior, shape our goals, offer a sense of direction, *and* help us to create meaning. In other words, meaning is related to the end of purpose. And as I suggested, finding purpose is a forward-looking activity, as opposed to meaning, which is temporally bound to our past. But finding purpose isn't something that can be done in a few days, weeks, or months. It will be a

[7] Steven C. Hayes (2004). Acceptance and Commitment Therapy, Relational Frame Theory, and the Third Wave of Behavioral and Cognitive Therapies, *Behavior Therapy*, 35, pp. 639–665.

life-long journey that can only be taken one step at a time. To discover our life's purpose, however, is the first step toward living a more conscious and meaningful life.

We may also discover that something that may have been meaningful to us at one point in our life changes over time. During our journey through life what we once perceived as our purpose may shift and change in response to the evolving priorities and fluctuations of our personal experiences. As I also mentioned before, meaning very much relies upon our memories of the past and our understanding of our present circumstances in order to provide us with a sense of unity, grounding, and comprehension. Often, we find (or make) meaning by revising or reappraising memories of past events and by connecting these past memories to present experiences and future possibilities. It is these connections between present and desired future events that guide our present actions. Meaning and purpose are separate, albeit highly related, constructs that build on one another to contribute to the broader concept of a "good" or meaningful life.

Discovering what's meaningful to us—having acquired a sense of purpose—doesn't mean all our problems will disappear, but at least we will have a general idea of what we want to get out of life. When we have a clearer sense of purpose, we can set the right goals and plans. We will be able to live lives that are congruent with our beliefs and values. We can live authentically. We can differentiate between what's important and unimportant and direct our energy to the really important things. And when we pursue whatever we believe is important, we will energize ourselves and be the best we can be.

I do realize that for some people, it's not easy to identify what they are really passionate about, what makes them feel truly alive. I have seen others, however, for whom a purpose and passion in life have always been obvious and clear. It is not difficult for these people to recognize their gifts. They are fortunate: they easily identify what they are good at, the talents they possess, and what gives them energy. They also derive much pleasure from honing these talents. As the German writer and statesman Johann Wolfgang von Goethe wrote, "The man who is born with a talent which he is meant to use, finds his greatest happiness in using it." Having a very special gift is rare, however. "*Wunderkinder*" are few and far between. Nevertheless, most of us have some interests and are attracted to a activities that give us energy and make us feel more alive. And what's more, doing what we enjoy doing—to engage in these kinds of activities—will give us a sense of control. Through persistent practice, we can even get better at doing the things that bring us enjoyment. These activities may also provide us with a sense of mastery. Eventually, whatever we are good at can evolve into meaningful, satisfying work. Other people might find their purpose in taking responsibility for their family or friends. For them, the community matters most. And then we find people who find meaning through spirituality or religious belief. Again, there are others who find their purpose clearly expressed in all these aspects of life. Whatever our purpose on the road to meaning, it will be a unique journey for each of us.

The journey of life is not about the destination but about exploration. During the journey, some beautiful paths will only be discovered when we get lost. Inevitably, there will be obstacles on the way. Some of the situations we encounter will fill us with joy, some with heartache. These periods of darkness are essential, however, in order to expand our personal awareness. Encounters with sadness and loss make us more appreciative of life. The only way not to make mistakes in life is to do nothing, which would be the greatest mistake of all. Thus, given the winding road we will be on, we may have to undergo many trials before we discover the right way to live and what makes our life meaningful. At the end of the day, there may be nothing but the journey, because the destination may turn out to be a pure illusion. Our mantra for this journey might well be "The journey is all, the end nothing."

As I have said repeatedly, the only way to find the answers we are looking for is to venture deeper within ourselves. Making this inner journey will provide us with new thoughts, ideas, and hopes. We shouldn't be surprised, however, that this journey may turn out to be the hardest we will ever undertake in our life. Nevertheless, while going on this inner journey, we should figure out what makes us laugh—and do more of it. We should figure out what makes us cry—and do less of it. And as the caterpillar needs to undergo a dramatic transformation within its cocoon before it emerges as a butterfly, likewise, this inner journey may have a great transformative impact.

11

Getting to the "How To"

Each man must look to himself to teach him the meaning of life. It is not something discovered: it is something molded.
—Antoine de Saint-Exupéry

People pay for what they do, and still more for what they have allowed themselves to become. And they pay for it very simply: by the lives they lead.
—James Baldwin

Turning once again to Ted, whose dilemma I began this book with—we saw how his existential angst gave him the motivation to figure out what *gave* meaning to his life and what was really important to him. It was Ted's experience of nothingness that led him to question the meaning of his existence. His challenge was how to go from nothingness to somethingness. His anxiety about the finiteness of life became the starting point for his search for authenticity, control, competence, belonging, purpose, community, and meaning. It encouraged him to question things he had previously not dared to question or pushed away from consciousness. Paradoxically, Ted's existential crisis helped him to gain greater insight about himself. It became the starting point of an exploratory journey that led him to discover what gave his life meaning and made his life more livable. His existential malaise enabled him to take responsibility for his life and to take meaningful action.

The tipping point moment for Ted was his decision to take time off and spend a weekend in the mountains with the only real friend he had left. The intense conversations that followed helped him to break out of his self-imposed prison and gave him the opportunity to reframe his situation. Taking

M. F. R. Kets de Vries, *Quo Vadis?*, The Palgrave Kets de Vries Library,
https://doi.org/10.1007/978-3-030-66699-6_11

time out from his day-to-day "busyness" made it possible for him to see things from a different perspective.

Ted concluded that wallowing in misery about the human condition—in particular his sense of futility and fear of death—wasn't very constructive. He came to realize that although humans can never escape from the reality of death, in the interim we can use our talents to create meaning. There are ways to transform our anxiety about our inevitable death. By building, loving, and creating, we can turn our life into a personal adventure.

Ted realized that whatever gave meaning to his life wouldn't come to him just by chance. He needed to take control of his life and make his own choices. It was up to him to pull himself out of his funk. It was up to him to create meaning. It was also his responsibility to create a sense of belonging. But to be able to do all these things, he needed to take an honest look at his life. In many ways, death is like a mirror in which the true meaning of life can be reflected. Looking at this mirror showed Ted his pains and pleasures, disappointments and desires. Only by looking into himself would he be able to work through his depressive thoughts, disappointments, regrets, anxieties, and feelings of being alone. The reflections in the mirror would help him accept who he really was, but he would only feel really alive through self-acceptance.

Ted had failed to pay attention to what was really going on in his life for far too long. Preferring not to see, he had closed his eyes to the fact that he disliked his work, that his marriage was on the rocks, and that he had alienated most of his friends. And although he had had success at work and still had a more or less amicable relationship with his wife, this was not enough to dissolve his emotional vacuum. By being dishonest with himself, he had worsened his concerns about authenticity, community, and meaning. But the past was the past. The present felt quite different. It screamed for action.

Ted's existential angst helped him to become more open to life's realities. The emotional void he found himself in made him decide to stop lying to himself and realize that it was high time to take greater control of his life. At the same time, he recognized that there was a positive side to his existential crisis. It had pushed him out of his comfort zone and helped him to reframe his present situation. It also made him realize that there is such a thing as free will but that it was up to him to take control over whatever he wanted to pursue. It was up to him to give his life purpose, value, and meaning, and up to him to be a participant rather than a mere observer of his own life. But if he wanted to make something meaningful out of his life, if he wanted to live life to the fullest, again, it was up to him not to let things drift. His major challenge was to find different ways of renewing himself, not to give up but to persevere in spite of life's absurdities. It was up to him to transcend his devastating feeling of meaninglessness into meaningfulness.

Ted had figured out that one of life's paradoxes is that we only come closer to ourselves when we stop running away. In other words, that we should avoid dying while we are living. With that in mind, and after some experimentation, Ted concluded that activities like self-development (in his case studying for a doctorate at the local university in a field that had always interested him), rebuilding his bonds with friends and family members, participating in community activities and dedicating time to spiritual matters, were the things that made him feel that he was truly alive. It was these activities that gave him energy. On his friend's recommendation, he also decided to take my modular workshop on leadership, a seminar that deals with issues of personal renewal. After the first module of the program he sent me the following email:

> *I have to tell you that I found the first week of the workshop a highly unusual learning experience: intellectually stimulating, emotionally confronting and above all, working within an ecosystem which allowed space for deep self-reflection and dare I say, self-discovery.*
>
> *As I was going through my own personal journey, what I found most intriguing was the evolution of the group's behavior, its changing dynamics and individual behaviors as the week progressed. Even more intriguing was the fact that by taking a step back to observe the group, I learned more about myself than I had in the last twenty plus years, particularly how I experience people and group situations. In addition, it also led me to discover many hard truths about myself.*
>
> *Through my colleague-participants' case presentations, I also learned a great deal of what makes people function. Your statement that "Everyone is normal until you know them better" really stuck with me. Listening to the various stories, it proved to be so true. Also, through the stories my fellow-participants told, I got a much deeper understanding of their personalities. I saw how all of us are so diverse and different from each other. At the same time, it became quite clear that we are also quite similar. Most of us have to deal with similar problems. And although I thought I knew something about people, the week of workshop took me into a much deeper dimension. I must admit that I find what I learned very hard to explain in words. It is more of some kind of feeling.*
>
> *I like to add that I very much recognized myself in others. It led to the dreaded realization of "Oh, my God, that's me!" "That's again me in that situation" or "Why did I act the way I did?" But the safe ecosystem allowed me to see myself in these different situations without having to visualize myself as a third person. It was like a third person was observing "me" in these various situations. This led to many weird déjà vu moments. But once I realized the value of the various interventions, I came to appreciate how the group afforded me with a unique learning experience, and I found I could fully immerse myself. I was able to do so, as the ambiance created by you felt quite safe.*

As a first step in his journey towards change, Ted decided that his marriage was important to him but also realized that he was running out of time to rebuild it. He would really have to try to make it work. He also resolved to make an effort to work on his friendships, which he had neglected for far too long. Another major decision he made was to quit his company. He needed to reassess what gave him energy—what kind of activities gave him pleasure. It was time to do something very different.

By taking all these decisions, Ted turned the corner from despair into hope. After having descended into what he later would describe as his lowest depths, he realized that he would only feel better in his skin if he had meaningful relations with others, engaged with a larger community of people, and could pursue activities he viewed as truly meaningful. He realized that what he really loved (and was very good at) was uplifting others. He liked to help people grow and develop. Mentorship made him feel more alive and authentic and gave him energy. They helped him to feel valued. By initiating these things, Ted had the feeling that he was making a difference, however small it might be. This change in his outlook turned out to be an effective way of coping with the narcissistic injury of the thought that time was running out. Eventually, Ted decided to sell his stake in his company to become involved in a small NGO aimed at educating handicapped children. This became his way to create meaning and transcend narrow, personal interests.

With Ted's example in mind, we may now have a better idea of the steps each of us can take to create a more meaningful life and be more mindful of the world around us. We may now recognize the truth of the statement that when we discover our why, the how will follow. This brings me to the question of what each of us can do to consciously design a life of meaning.

There are five pillars of "being" that influence the way we experience meaning: belonging, purpose, competence, control and transcendence. I have touched on all of these throughout this book. I call the grouping of these five pillars an "authentizotic" orientation, a term I devised by combining two Greek words, *authentikos* (authenticity) and *zootikos* (vital to life). *Authentikos* implies a state of mind and way of living that contributes to the sense of effectiveness, competence, autonomy, and creativity. *Zootikos* describes the way our need for balance, commitment, completeness, and exploration is met (see an overview of the five pillars in Fig. 11.1).

Furthermore, to help my clients assess how effectively they deal with the five dimensions that make up meaning, I devised the *Meaning in Life Questionnaire* (see Fig. 11.2). It is meant to make a quick assessment of which of the five pillars they may need to work on. Subsequently, a deep dive will be needed to understand why that's the case—what is their story all about.

Our Existential Challenges

Fig. 11.1 Existential challenges

7—strongly agree
6—agree
5—slightly agree
4—neither agree or disagree
3—slightly disagree
2—disagree
1—strongly disagree

p__ I am leading a very purposeful life.

c__ My life is full of interesting learning experiences.

b__My interactions with other people give me a lot of pleasure.

co__It is up to me to make something of my life.

p__I look forward to the new, exciting challenges that each day come my way.

c__I very much enjoy what I am doing.

co__ I feel free to make whatever life choices.

b__I have a very fulfilling social network.

t__When I die, I believe that I have led a very worthwhile life.

c__I can completely lose myself in whatever I do.

b__I am very close to my family and friends.

co__I feel very much in control of my life.

p__I have always been very effective in pursuing my life's goals.

t__I get a lot of pleasure out of helping others.

t__I am actively involved in dealing with issues that are larger than me.

Fig. 11.2 Meaning in Life Questionnaire

Scoring

Add up your responses. The range of scores is from 15 (lowest possible) to 105 (highest possible). A high score suggests that you have many psychological resources and strengths. A low score indicates that work needs to be done on the various dimensions of meaning. (Key: b=belonging; p=purpose; c=competence; co=control; t=transcendence).

Telling Our Story

To create a meaningful life, these five pillars need to be woven into a compelling personal narrative. We should be able to tell a story that explains our role in our life's journey. Storytelling is an innate human impulse that reflects the way we tend to think. The stories we tell, and the way we tell them, reveal who we are and become an essential part of ourselves. The ability to tell our story will help us to enact whatever we're doing. Stories give us a sense of direction and a purpose. Our challenge is to create a life that contains a story worth telling.

We should also remember that the story we tell doesn't come from nowhere. It is based on our salient experiences and provides us with an identity. As story tellers, we create our own personal myths that contain heroes and villains, people who have helped us or held us back, major events that determine the plot, challenges that we have overcome and suffering we have endured.

By and large, when we tell our story we are likely to focus on the most extraordinary good and bad events in our life. These are the experiences we need to make sense of, the trials and tribulations that help us understand what has shaped us, the things that tell us what's really significant. Taking the disparate pieces of our lives and putting them together into a coherent narrative allows us to understand our life as a whole. And as our personal narrative provides us with an identity, it embeds us within something bigger than ourselves. While telling our story, we realize that we are part of a greater entity. From a legacy perspective, we should see our stories as a gift to future generations.

In addition, stories help us to connect the past and present to the future. In telling our story, we will be able to transform ourselves, learn about our history and recount our experiences as a way of transcending them. Storytelling also helps us to broaden our perspective to see further than usual. It gives us the opportunity to act beyond a narrative that once may have imprisoned us and help us attain our full potential. The way our story evolves will give meaning to all our experiences and choices.

While we tell our story, our meaning making may resonate with others. And an even more significant kind of meaning will be created when several people weave together a common network of stories, as happened in the workshop in which Ted participated.

What's sometimes not recognized is that the story we tell others may contain implicit aspects of our lives without our conscious awareness. Again, it will be our challenge to make these unconscious aspects, conscious. This kind of activity becomes a highly effective way to explore out-of-awareness behavior. In fact, storytelling can be a primary way through which we not only communicate meaning to others, but also explore often-hidden content in our search for meaning.

The power of storytelling explains why journal writing and intimate communication with others—which are often narrative processes—can have such powerful organizing effects on our mind and a positive impact on our physical well-being. Keeping a journal allows us to express overwhelming emotions and observe our thought patterns, rather than simply reacting to them. Recording the small details of our daily life can help us to feel more grounded, more connected. We may better understand our own history, put our past into context, and make sense of experiences that previously might not have made sense to us. Thus, the act of writing helps us to prioritize our problems, fears, and concerns. Also, it allows us to track patterns, trends, improvement,and growth over time.

All of us need to find a unique narrative of our life's significant events and moments. And how we present our story to the outside should be congruent with the story that's evolving within. A rupture only contributes to the feeling of inauthenticity.

Transcendence

Life is more than having great sex, owning a mansion, driving a nice car, or having a yacht, and those for whom this is not obvious better realize that quickly. We need to make an effort to transcend that kind of materialism. I have stressed throughout this book that living a full, meaningful life depends on how we connect with our community and family, how we can contribute usefully to society, and how we can engage in various forms of self-improvement, with the purpose of being helpful to others.

This kind of self-improvement program, as I suggested before, doesn't mean that we have to be grandiose in our search for meaning. The process of meaning-making might just boil down to finding one or two things that are bigger than ourselves and bigger than those around us. After all, how many people receive the Nobel Peace Prize? How many people turn out to be a Nelson Mandela? However, each of us can make an effort—modest though such an effort may be—to give our best during the time we have on this earth. Clearly, the purpose of life—and what turns purpose into meaning—is to make a positive impact. Thus, each day, whenever possible, *we should try to make a difference in someone's life, including our own.* By engaging in activities that create meaning, each of us can make a small difference to this world. Those activities can take many different shapes, for example, giving advice to a friend, engaging in artistic endeavors that others will enjoy, helping students to solve their problems, or simply, bringing some joy into the life of someone else. And while we're doing all these things, we should create happy moments for ourselves. There is nothing wrong about enjoying the strawberries or lick the honey.

Looking for "Flow"

In our pursuit of meaning-making, we cannot expect a "eureka" moment, to wake up one morning and suddenly know exactly what we should do with our life. We will only discover what constitutes meaning for us through trial and error. To get to that point, we have to ask ourselves a number of questions, like what do I love doing? What comes easily to me? And what gives me flow?

Flow experiences happen when we are completely concentrated on the task at hand, to the extent that we lose track of time. Haven't we all have had this sense of "flow?" Haven't we all got so involved in an activity that minutes turned into hours and hours turned into "I can't believe what time it is."[1] When we are in "flow," we are not sidetracked by other thoughts. We are functioning at our optimal performance level. And when we are in such a mental state, nothing else matters. The goals and rewards are clear. It's like we have a direct feedback loop and know how well we are doing. Time becomes meaningless when we are in a state of flow. Whatever we're doing, it appears effortless and easy as we have a sense of control over the task at hand.

If you have had flow experiences, in which you feel truly alive and the best you can be, you should look at the circumstances and conditions under which they occur, even if it's something like chopping wood. The rational side of your brain may think it meaningless, but a state of flow can turn out to hold important hidden meanings.

Another helpful question we can ask ourselves is what we would be doing if we knew that we couldn't fail at it? What would we do even if we weren't paid

[1] Mihaly Csikszentmihalyi (2008). *Flow: The Psychology of Optimal Experience.* New York: Harper Perennial Modern Classics.

to do it? These questions help us to tease out whether we are where we really like to be. Are we on the right track? Are we spending time on activities that really suit us? Or are we doing things other people want us to do? I can make the same observation about our relationships. Are our relationships what we want them to be? Could they be deeper, more rewarding, more meaningful?

In our pursuit of a meaningful life, we would do well to take a hard look at the kinds of people we deal with. The people we surround ourselves with say something about us. Why we have chosen them? Do they give us energy—adding to our sense of flow—or are they draining? We should steer clear of toxic people, individuals who are incompatible with what we expect from others. We should avoid the kinds of people that try to drag us down. After all, it is quite difficult to feel passionate and purposeful when we're surrounded by people who aren't interested in making positive contributions. The less we deal with negative people, the more we will succeed in our pursuit of meaning. Instead, it is imperative to look for people who help us to be our best.

Keeping all these factors in mind, we may discover that some people will only be with us for part of our journey through life. Others may grow with us, to continue to bring meaning to our lives. Clearly, if we surround ourselves with people who lead meaningful lives, they are likely to inspire us to do something similar. We need both dreamers and doers in our life, people who recognize our talents, particularly if we haven't yet have recognized them ourself.

Pay Attention to the "Stealth Motivator"

There's nothing we can do about birth and death except enjoy the interval. We all move between these two unknowns. But when the end comes, we need to be able to say, "I didn't waste my time. I didn't go silently into that good night." Only by imagining our non-existence can we get a sense of what is most important about our existence. Death creates scarcity in our life, giving whatever activities we choose to spend time on meaning and value. Death is a stealth motivator, and we need to pay attention to it.

As time would become meaningless if there were too much of it, we should not waste our time on things that don't give our life meaning. To quote Seneca, "Begin at once to live and count each day as a separate life." It will be too late to ask ourselves why we lived the life we did and what we would do if we had our time again on our deathbed. Instead, we should try to live in the here and now as fully and creatively as we can. As I have learned from experience, once we accept the inevitability of our own death, we suddenly feel much freer to live. The stealth motivator invites us to live life to the fullest and warns us not to waste our time. It is our mortality that gives meaning, depth and poignancy to the way we live.

We could also ask ourselves what we would do if we had only a year left to live. What would my obituary look like? What would my legacy be? Again, these questions force us to zero in on what's really meaningful in our lives and what's just empty busyness. And we need to live the answers. While reflecting on what we should spend our time and energy on, we may realize that it's very hard to obtain some things in life, like love, truth, kindness, and imagination. Without meaning, life can become a real tragedy.

"Dare to err and dare to dream"

The German playwright, Friedrich Schiller, wrote, "Dare to err and to dream. I have often seen how deep meaning can often be found in childish plays." In my work, I have seen how often play can be a highly effective way to reveal meaning, even though it may come to us in very subtle ways. Often, play contains indications of what our destiny is going to be. It tells us something about the activities that make us feel truly alive.

Unfortunately, as the years go by, many of us may lose touch with the things that we loved to do when we were children. For too many of us, our passions our squeezed out by the pressure to conform. Societal expectations force us to show a false self.[2] When we live a life that's dictated by others it is hard to find the purpose of our own life. Not surprisingly, people commonly follow the ideals that other people instill in them and fail to follow their own heart's desires. Far too many people never take control of their own life. And far too many people are swayed by what they think they should do, rather than what they really want to do. If too many of our activities are based on what others think, we are not going in the right direction.

If our reasons for not doing what we really want to do is that others wouldn't approve, or worse, make fun of us, it's time to rethink our situation. There will be a real possibility that, without realizing it, we are trying to live the life of others. Again, to prevent this from happening, we should remind ourselves of what we loved to do when we were children. What do our dreams and day-dreams tell us? Where and when do we feel happiest? And what do we do most naturally and effortlessly?

[2] Donald W. Winnicott (1960). Ego distortion in terms of true and false self. *The Maturational Process and the Facilitating Environment: Studies in the Theory of Emotional Development*. New York: International Universities Press, Inc., pp. 140–57.

Identifying or recognizing what's truly our passion always starts with a sense of play. When we start examining our lives through play, we can see what's truly important to us, what drives us, and, especially, what makes us feel truly alive. As might be expected, when we follow our passions, we have no choice but to leave our comfort zone. Often, meaning comes from the unknown or unpredictable. Taking this step may be difficult for many of us, as our greatest enemy is complacency. We get stuck in routines very easily. Although we may have found many ways to distract ourselves—to attach ourselves to these routines—we should remind ourselves that it is the challenge of doing different things that makes life truly interesting. But again, it is up to us to choose. We have the freedom to do so, how unnerving making choices can be, at times. We should never forget, however, it is up to us to own our own life. And it is the choices we make that will determine whether we live a meaningful life. Whatever we decide to focus on, it is the only life we will ever have.

The Ouroboros: The Inner Journey

The ouroboros is an ancient symbol that represents a serpent or dragon eating its own tail, variously signifying infinity and the cycle of life, death, and rebirth. It is a symbol of eternal cyclical renewal, the tail of the snake being a phallic symbol, and the mouth being a yonic or womb-like symbol. The image of the ouroboros brings me once again to the question that runs like a red thread throughout this book: how can we reinvent ourselves so that we stay truly alive and avoid a living death? As must be clear by now, the answer to that question is the pursuit of meaning. But it must also be clear by now that finding meaning isn't a given.

If we want our lives to have depth and meaning, we need to be present, mindful, and live with intention. We need to make a conscious effort to figure out what we are all about. Throughout this book I have stressed that this means being prepared to undertake an inner journey—to face our inner demons, and know the strengths, weaknesses, values, and beliefs that justify our actions. Through this inner journey, we can create maps of meaning for ourselves. Conversely, if we take a reactive stand and just wait and see, we aren't going to get the answer. In other words, either we move the world, or the world will move us. If we don't show the world why we were born, the world will show us why we were born—but we won't necessarily like what we see.

Finding a Guide

Ted's experiences in recognizing and working through his existential crisis have been another red thread we have followed through earlier chapters. Ted was fortunate to have a good friend who pushed him to participate in my workshop, which has a very clinical orientation and is a form of accelerated form of psychotherapy. Most of us who struggle with existential crises need this kind of support and many will need the help of a psychotherapist.

Most therapeutic work that deals with the existential dilemmas of the human condition is focused on the here-and-now (especially within the transferential relationship with the psychotherapist). Given the great impact of transferential processes—how past experiences will influence future behavior and actions—psychodynamically oriented psychotherapists focus on these past life experiences.[3] To be more precise, psychotherapists are always aware of these possible confusions in time and place. In its most simple terms, clients may react to some people as if they are representative of important people from their past who influence the way of looking at things. For psychotherapists and coaches with a psychodynamic orientation, transference is a helpful process to better understand the scripts in their clients' inner theater and what drives them. These kinds of psychotherapeutic exchanges focus not only on "being" but also "becoming."

In my role as a psychoanalyst, psychotherapist, and coach, my challenge is to encourage my clients to take ownership of their complaints. I need to help them see that their way of being is something they may have chosen, but that they have the freedom to choose better ways of coping—ways that will give more meaning to their lives. It is up to them, however, to take control over their own life.

When I put on my helping professional's hat, I want to help my clients find out what really matters to them and help them locate themselves in the world within the parameters and limits of their capabilities. Also, I focus on explaining the limitations of the human condition. This means that my clients have to face up to their concerns about death, suffering, guilt, anger, regret, freedom, isolation, loneliness, and meaninglessness. They also have to accept the paradox that life's absence of meaning creates the need for meaning to replace existential anxiety and guilt.

My interventions depend on my understanding of my clients' worldview and the state of mind (their values and belief systems). For example, I explore their current issues and concerns and try to put the issues that trouble them into perspective. I also explore their background and how it affects their

---

[3] Heinrich Racker (2001). *Transference and Countertransference*, New York: International Universities Press.

present behavior. Apart from the psychodynamics at play, a systemic orientation is also a sine qua non for truly understanding what's happening to them. I help them see life's paradoxes and guide them to come to terms with them.

I also want my clients to address their inner demons—their dark side—without resorting to denial or distortion. While doing so, I challenge them by having them think through the consequences of their choices (both past and future); having them recognize and accept their limitations as well as their possibilities; having them take responsibility for their choices; encouraging them to fulfill their potentiality for being; and having them become the master of their own fate. In addressing these issues, I try to help my clients to find purpose and motivation and find out what is truly meaningful to them.

Looking into the Mirror, Darkly

As you will have realized by now, there is no easy answer to the question, what's the meaning of life? It's probably the wrong question to ask. The real question should be, what is the meaning of *my* life? As the writer, Anais Nin once said, "There is not one big cosmic meaning for all; there is only the meaning we give to our life, an individual meaning, an individual plot, like an individual novel, a book for each person." Each of us has the responsibility to bring meaning to our life, not wait for life to bring us meaning. Our challenge is to live the tragic transience of our days with passion and, when the curtain falls, to make a good exit. And to ensure the quality of that exit, we should be able to look back on something enduring to which we have contributed by creating something beyond ourselves.

But as the meaning of life will always be a very personal matter, it could appear like a rainbow on the horizon. We will never be able to touch it, but what's more important are our attempts to get closer to it. These are the endeavors that will give value to our life. Whatever we accomplish when trying to reach this rainbow will be our greatest legacy. And when our curtain comes down, an important question will be whether we will leave this life with the quieting thought that we have been able to contribute to the wellness of many who will live after us.

Furthermore, the art of living also implies that we need to accept that life cannot be lived and death cannot be faced without experiencing anxiety over our temporary stay on this earth. This is the knowledge that has made for the tragic quality of human existence since we evolved a thinking brain. It is the knowledge that drove us out of the Garden of Eden. It is also what makes us realize that the real tragedy of our life isn't death, but the discovery that we may have never really lived when the time comes for us to die. Shakespeare, in his play *Macbeth*, lays bare the existential anguish of the human condition:

> Life's but a walking shadow, a poor player
> That struts and frets his hour upon the stage
> And then is heard no more. It is a tale
> Told by an idiot, full of sound and fury,
> Signifying nothing.[4]

But if we embrace life—if we recognize its paradoxes, predicaments, and problems—we will be better prepared to face death. If we realize that we can make choices—that it is up to us to live life authentically—we will be better prepared for the end of that life. Furthermore, if we assume the responsibility to live in a way that's consistent with our true nature and core values—in spite of the risks, setbacks and suffering that such a journey may entail—we will feel better in our skin. And if we also accept that suffering is part of the human condition, we will be more prepared to carry ourselves beyond despair. People who live life meaningfully fear death less. Their personal transcendence is their way of attaining something that resembles immortality. As Shakespeare also wrote, in a different context, "The readiness is all."

---

[4] https://www.sparknotes.com/nofear/shakespeare/macbeth/page_202/ act 5, scene 5

Index

M. F. R. Kets de Vries, *Quo Vadis?*, The Palgrave Kets de Vries Library,
https://doi.org/10.1007/978-3-030-66699-6

Ingram Content Group UK Ltd.
Milton Keynes UK
UKHW022114220623
423898UK00009B/924